ਸ੍ਰੀ ਵਾਹਿਗੁਰੂ ਜੀ ਕੀ ਫਤਹ ॥

ਸ੍ਰੀ ਭਵਾਨੀ ਜੀ ਸਹਾਇ ॥

ਸ੍ਰੀ ਆਯਾ ਲਛਮੀ ਜੀ ਸਹਾਇ ॥

Contents

Introduction

**Philosophical Underpinnings & Key
Considerations**

Piri

As with all things related to temporal affairs, attention must be given to the spiritual in the beginning. For this reason, the introduction to this manifesto will attempt to first establish the philosophical underpinnings upon which the rest of the economic and political ideology that is Azadism will be based on. Without at least some level of spiritual progress this manifesto is useless, and the reader is better off reading Gurbani or doing Simran until a necessary state of competency is obtained. Where that level will be is entirely subjective, something that only the reader and their Guru can know. This manifesto has been designed primarily for a Khalsa audience, however not exclusively. A base level commitment to both Sant and Sipahi nature is assumed on behalf of the reader. Whilst the majority of this publication will be based in *Miri*, this introduction will briefly outline the *Piri* aspects necessary before delving further.

To help to ground these concepts and reconcile the economic aspects with Sikhi, throughout the course of this manifesto the spiritual components will constantly be referred back to in the form of Bani and Ithiaas. This introduction will begin with a Sakhi from Shaheed Bhai Mani Singh's 'Sikhan Di Bhagat Mala'[1], however before this it is imperative to understand what exactly *Ithiaas* is. Whilst generically, it is commonly used as a term for history, this definition falls short. Instead, Ithiaas is a combination of three components:

> **History** - Events which actually occurred in the past
> **Mythology** - The embellishment and sensationalism of events that may or may not have happened
> **Reality** - How the story is applicable to your own life today

To say Ithiaas is just history misses the mark. In Ithiaas, the historicity of events is secondary to the actual message, or moral of the story. Unless you were actually there, experiencing an event for yourself, you can never truly know all the details of what happened. Nor do you need to. Whilst effort can be spent on determining archaeological records or gathering eye-witness accounts, this will always be less important nor as useful compared to actually understanding the point of the story. Imagine spending your life looking for Noah's Ark, as opposed to understanding the moral implications and deep wisdom of the story. This story is not unique to Christianity either, as it has similar counterparts in more ancient traditions and texts like the Epic of Gilgamesh, or the story of the Saptarishi and Manu in Hindu tradition. Even our own Sikh traditions are full of these stories, with Guru Gobind Singh even writing his own version of the Ramayan, emphasising the Bir Ras more so than in any other version before it. Whilst these events may have happened, and these stories based on true events, that is only ever secondary to the point or feeling the authors are aiming to represent by them. Mythological references are borrowed and implanted to help connect with the reader and build a sense of awe and make it memorable. Therefore, Ithiaas is a combination of both history and mythology as it is meant to act like a vessel for wisdom and knowledge. It is easier to relate to deep spiritual concepts through a story since we can build personal connections with the characters and events. So much so that those events map onto our own experiences. Sita becomes a metaphor for the self and the distraction in the form the golden deer is Maya. The subsequent separation from her beloved Raam Chandar is analogous to our own separation between the Atma and Paramatma[2]. This is when the final component - reality - completes the definition of *Ithiaas*.

During the time of Guru Arjan Dev, four Sikhs approached the Guru seeking answers to an issue they were having regarding the question of free-will. They presented the Guru with his Bani saying that in some places he suggests that the individual has no autonomy over their own actions:

ਮਰੈ ਰਾਖੈ ਏਕੋ ਆਪਿ ॥ ਮਾਨੁਖ ਕੈ ਕਛੁ ਨਾਹੀ ਹਾਥਿ ॥

Preservation and destruction both are done by the One; there is nothing in the hands of the individual.

— Sri Guru Granth Sahib, Ang 281

3

However in other places he suggests the opposite and encourages control over one's actions:

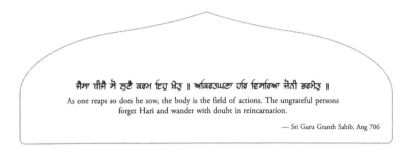

ਜੈਸਾ ਬੀਜੈ ਸੋ ਲੁਣੈ ਕਰਮ ਇਹੁ ਖੇਤੁ ॥ ਅਕਿਰਤਘਣਾ ਹਰਿ ਵਿਸਰਿਆ ਜੋਨੀ ਭਰਮੇਤੁ ॥

As one reaps so does he sow, the body is the field of actions. The ungrateful persons forget Hari and wander with doubt in reincarnation.

— Sri Guru Granth Sahib, Ang 706

They tell the Guru that if God themselves do everything then what can be attributed to us as a cause of actions? Which of these positions is true and which should be rejected? The above are just examples from the Sakhi, however Panktis from all over Bani can be used to show this paradox. Notably, Japu ji Sahib has a few examples of this, where parts talk of Hukam being in control of everything, nothing is outside of it; or there is no effort that can be made by an individual, only God can apply effort. Whereas other parts, including the concluding Salok reminds us of the importance of actions in getting closer or further to God. The Guru responds in this way:

ਜੋ ਗੁਰਾਂ ਦੇ ਗਿਰੰਥ ਜੀ ਦੇ ਵਿਚ ਸਭਟਾ ਆਧਕਾਰ ਦੇ ਵਚਨ ਹੈਨ ॥ ਤੇ ਗੁਰੂ ਕੇ ਸਿਖ ਭੀ ਸਭਨਾ ਆਧਕਾਰਾ ਦੇ ਹੈਨ ॥

The sayings within the Guru Granth Ji are all associated with one's particular competency, and the Sikhs of the Guru represent all levels of competency.

ਇਕ ਕਰਮਾ ਦੇ ਆਧਕਾਰੀ ਹੁੰਦੇ ਹੈਨ ॥ ਤੇ ਜੇਹੜੇ ਕਰਮਾ ਦੇ ਆਧਕਾਰੀ ਹੈਨ ਉਨਾ ਪ੍ਰਤੀ ਏਹੁ ਵਚਨ : ਜੈਸਾ ਬੀਜੈ ਸੋ ਲੁਣੈ ਕਰਮ ਇਹੁ ਖੇਤੁ ॥

One level of competency is related to Karma, and to those who are in the competency of Karma, for those persons this saying is appropriate:
"As one reaps so does he sow, the body is the field of actions."

ਜੇਹੜੇ ਉਪਾਸਨਾ ਦੇ ਆਧਕਾਰੀ ਹੈਨ ॥ ਉਨਾਪ੍ਰਤਿ ਏਹੁ ਬਚਨ ਹੈਨ : ਕਰੇ ਕਰਾਵੈ ਆਪੇ ਆਪ ॥

Those who are the competency of Devotional worship [Upashana], for those persons this saying is appropriate:
"Prabhu himself is the Cause of all Causes."

ਜੋ ਗਿਆਨ ਦੇ ਆਧਕਾਰੀ ਹੈਨ ਉਨਾਪ੍ਰਤਿ ਏਹੁ ਬਚਨ ਹੈਨ : ਘਟਘਟਿ ਅੰਤਰ ਸਰਬ ਨਿਰੰਤਰ ਹਰਿ ਏਕੋ ਪੁਰਖ ਸਮਾਣਾ ॥

For those who are the competency of Wisdom, for those persons this saying is appropriate:
"Within each and every heart you are Omni-present, Hari is the One Being merged with all."

— Words of Sri Guru Arjan Dev, Sikhan Di Bhagat Mala

The Guru outlines not two, but three possible positions in the free-will vs determinism debate. For someone on the spiritual competency of "karma" (action), then those areas of Bani that speak to individual effort and free-will is appropriate. For someone who is an Upashik, those Shabads that emphasise devotion and love become paramount. However, what is the difference between Upashana and Gyaan (Wisdom)? Both the level of Karma and Upashana maintain a separate sense of self. The duality between the individual and God remains in both these levels since these states require an individual to do some effort of their own free-will. This perhaps may be easier to understand for someone at the competency of Karma since they still hold a sense of self in order to do right or wrong actions. Those actions or karma "attach" to that self, and so a separate ego is still necessary. Here you can assign blame or praise for someone's actions, as those actions conceptually "belong" to someone. For an Upashik, they still remain separate too, since in order to say to God that "you do everything", this still implies an "I and You" relationship. The only difference here is that through saying this and internalising it, the Upashik is in progress of reaching the final stage whereas those only concerned with action don't seem to escape duality as long as they are at that level. Therefore, the competency of Upashana can be seen as a transitory state, taking someone from the level of action (and perhaps ritual too) to the level of wisdom. It is only at the level of wisdom where the sense of a separate self breaks down completely. Here it is then understood that God *is* everything.

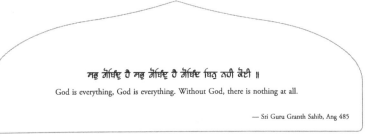

ਸਭੁ ਗੋਬਿੰਦੁ ਹੈ ਸਭੁ ਗੋਬਿੰਦੁ ਹੈ ਗੋਬਿੰਦ ਬਿਨੁ ਨਹੀ ਕੋਈ ॥

God is everything, God is everything. Without God, there is nothing at all.

— Sri Guru Granth Sahib, Ang 485

Everything includes yourself. The body, mind and soul are all God's. This doesn't mean that "you" belong to "God" now as if it is something separate - there is no "you"! The whole language of I, me, you, them (Haumai) is no longer applicable since it is all one thing. Existence itself. Since there is no self at this level, what can there be to exhibit any sort of free-will? At this point it is only God's will that can exist, only Hukam. The question of free will vs determinism is intrinsically linked to the concept of Ik Onkaar in this way. The answer of whether there is free will or not depends on the perspective of the individual (or lack thereof) asking the question.

It is almost guaranteed that much of what was just said would have gone over many readers heads, and that's okay. The Guru realises the reality that everyone is on different stages of understanding with these concepts. Guru Gobind Singh in his 'Gobind Gita', links these three levels of competency and applies a hierarchy of progression[3].

ਤਿਸ ਕੋ ਕਰਮ ਜੋਗ ਪਰਵਾਨ ॥ ਜੈਸੇ ਭਾਖੀ ਸ੍ਰੀ ਭਗਵਾਨ ॥ ਕਰਮ ਕਰਤ ਅੰਤਰ ਸੁਧ ਹੋਵੈ ॥ ਤਬ ਵਹੁ ਭਗਤਿ ਮਾਹਿ ਚਿਤ ਪੋਵੈ ॥੬੨॥

This method of Action [Karam] is acceptable, that which was instructed by Sri Bhagvan [Krishna]. By performing good actions [Karam] purity is achieved within oneself. Then a devotional spirit will reside within one's consciousness

ਭਗਤ ਕਰੈ ਤਬ ਪ੍ਰੇਮ ਹਰਿ ਪਾਵੈ ॥ ਪ੍ਰੇਮ ਕੀਏ ਗਿਆਨ ਗੁਨ ਗਾਵੈ ॥ ਗਿਆਨ ਤੇ ਜਾਨੈ ਅਪਨਾ ਰੂਪ ॥ ਚਿਰੰਕਾਲ ਵਹੁ ਬ੍ਰਹਮ ਸਰੂਪ ॥੬੩॥

By performing devotional service Love for Hari is realized, with this Love one recites the virtues and Wisdom [of Hari]. By having the Awareness [Gyaan, of Hari] one fully understands Oneself; which is what you were, that form of Braham, from the very beginning

ਜੋ ਇਹ ਗਿਆਨ ਕੋਊ ਲੇ ਧਾਰੇ ॥ ਏਕ ਬ੍ਰਹਮ ਅਦ੍ਵੈਤ ਚੀਨ੍ਹਾਰੇ ॥ ਅਦ੍ਵੈਤ ਮਾਹਿ ਦੂਸਰ ਨਹੀ ਕੋਇ ॥ ਅਬ ਹੀ ਬ੍ਰਹਮ ਆਪਿ ਵਹੁ ਹੋਇ ॥੬੪॥

Whoever has this awareness [Gyaan] instilled within their mind, they solely contemplate the Non-Dual Braham. They are absorbed in this Non-Dual; they recognize no other. In this way one becomes [One] with Braham

ਜੋ ਸੇਵੈ ਸੋਈ ਕਛੁ ਪਾਵੈ ॥ ਸੋਈ ਹੋਇ ਜਿਸ ਸੋ ਚਿਤੁ ਲਾਵੈ ॥ ਆਗੇ ਭੀ ਗੁਰ ਨਾਨਕ ਗਾਇਆ ॥ ਵਹੀ ਪ੍ਰਾਪਤਿ ਮਹ ਜਿਸ ਸੋ ਲਾਇਆ ॥੬੫॥

Whatever you serve you will become; you will become what you place your attention upon. This was sung before by Guru Nanak; from Him I have received this [knowledge] which I have presented

— Sri Guru Gobind Singh, Gobind Gita, Chapter 2

By first performing good action an inner "purity" is achieved, which acts as a basis to perform loving devotion. Love is an important attribute in spiritual progression since it is a paradoxical human behaviour that drives a person to overcome their self preservation instincts engrained over millions of years of evolution. Only in love does something other than the self get placed above one's own well-being. Love provides the necessary conditions in which to dissociate with the sense of self and attain oneness. The inclination to serve one's own interests is greatly inhibited during this stage of spiritual progression until a point is reached where there is a complete and successful ego-death, leaving only God left. Only God therefore is at the competency of Gyaan.

Returning to the original Sakhi, Guru Arjan Dev elaborates further on their approach to disseminating knowledge:

ਜੈਸੇ ਵੈਦ ਕੇ ਘਰ ਸਰਬ ਅਉਖਧ ਹੋਤੇ ਹੈਨ ॥ ਗਰਮੀ ਦੇ ਤਾਪ ਦਾ ਸਰਦੀ ਦੇ ਤਾਪ ਦਾ ਠੰਡ ਦੇ ਤਾਪ ਅਉਖਧ ਭਿੰਨ ਭਿੰਨ ਹੋਤਾ ਹੈ ॥

Just as in a doctor's office there are many different diseases present; just as a fever of warmth, cold weather, and a cold fever, there are numerous varieties of illnesses.

ਤੈਸੇ ਵੈਦ ਰੋਗੀ ਕੀ ਨਾਟਕਾ ਲਖੀ ਦੇਖ ਕਰ ਜੈਸਾ ਤਾਪ ਹੋਤਾ ਹੈ ਤੈਸਾ ਅਉਖਧ ਦੇਤੇ ਹੈ ॥ ਤਾ ਰੋਗੀ ਕਾ ਰੋਗ ਕਟਿਆ ਜਾਤਾ ਹੈ ॥

In this manner, a doctor in looking at the pulse and fluids prescribes the appropriate medicine for that illness, and through this manner he alleviates the illness that is suffered by the ill patient.

ਤੇ ਜੋ ਅਗਿਆਨ ਵੈਦ ਹੋਤਾ ਹੈ ਤਾ ਰੋਗੁ ਕਟਿਆ ਨਹੀ ਜਾਤਾ ॥ ਰੋਗ ਅਵਰ ਹੋਤਾ ਹੈ ਅਰ ਅਉਖਧ ਔਰ ਕਰਤਾ ਹੈ ॥

An uneducated doctor will not be able to relieve the illness of the patient. The illness will be of one kind and he will prescribe an irrelevant medicine.

ਤੈਸੇ ਸੰਤ ਜਨ ਜੋ ਹੈਨ ਪ੍ਰਭੁ ਕੇ ਵਚਨਾ ਦੁਆਰੇ ਅਰ ਕਰਮਾ ਦੁਆਰੇ ਪਛਾਣਦੇ ਹੈਨ ॥ ਰਸਨਾ ਦੁਆਰੇ ਹਿਰਦੇ ਕਾ ਮਤ ਮਲੂਮ ਹੋਦਾ ਹੈ ॥

In this manner, the Saints and Servants [of Hari] pay attention to the words and actions [of the Sikh]. In looking at their words, they come to know the inner understanding of their heart.

— Words of Sri Guru Arjan Dev, Sikhan Di Bhagat Mala

The Guru assesses each of his Sikh's individually, similarly to how a trained doctor also looks at each individual on a case-by-case basis. Just like the doctor, the Guru will not just prescribe only one type of teaching for the Sikhs, since he realises that humanity is diverse and each individual is unique. Hence why they are known as *Jagat* Guru. There is Sikhiya given dependent on each circumstance and relevant to all no matter what stage they are at.

This is also why the Guru can hold so many seemingly contradictory positions simultaneously in Bani. It is because not all of the concepts and teachings mentioned are completely relevant at each stage. Another example is reincarnation and karma. Only if you accept a sense of separateness can this work, otherwise on the level of wisdom, it's God themselves accruing the karma and going through a cycle of rebirth. If you have no free-will then it is not up to you whether you will enter this cycle since there is no you in the first place to be blamed for the karma you collect. Nonetheless, the Guru still uses this concept many times throughout Gurbani. Repeated mention of the 8.4 Million species life cycle is apparent throughout Sri Guru Granth Sahib.

ਲਖ ਚਉਰਾਸੀਹ ਭ੍ਰਮਤਿਆ ਦੁਲਭ ਜਨਮੁ ਪਾਇਓਇ ॥

Through 8.4 million incarnations you have wandered, to obtain this rare and precious human life.

ਨਾਨਕ ਨਾਮੁ ਸਮਾਲਿ ਤੂੰ ਸੋ ਦਿਨੁ ਨੇੜਾ ਆਇਓਇ ॥੪॥੨੨॥੯੨॥

O Nanak, remember the Naam, the Name of the Lord; the day of departure is drawing near! ||4||22||92||

— Sri Guru Granth Sahib, Ang 50

However, now consider this Bani from Bhagat Trilochan Ji in Raag Gujri:

ਅੰਤਿ ਕਾਲਿ ਜੋ ਲਛਮੀ ਸਿਮਰੈ ਐਸੀ ਚਿੰਤਾ ਮਹਿ ਜੇ ਮਰੈ ॥

At the very last moment, one who thinks of wealth, and dies in such thoughts,

ਸਰਪ ਜੋਨਿ ਵਲਿ ਵਲਿ ਅਉਤਰੈ ॥੧॥

shall be reincarnated over and over again, in the form of serpents. ||1||

ਅਰੀ ਬਾਈ ਗੋਬਿਦ ਨਾਮੁ ਮਤਿ ਬੀਸਰੈ ॥ ਰਹਾਉ ॥

O sister, do not forget the Name of the Lord of the Universe. ||Pause||

ਅੰਤਿ ਕਾਲਿ ਜੋ ਇਸਤ੍ਰੀ ਸਿਮਰੈ ਐਸੀ ਚਿੰਤਾ ਮਹਿ ਜੇ ਮਰੈ ॥

At the very last moment, he who thinks of women, and dies in such thoughts,

ਬੇਸਵਾ ਜੋਨਿ ਵਲਿ ਵਲਿ ਅਉਤਰੈ ॥੨॥

shall be reincarnated over and over again as a prostitute. ||2||

ਅੰਤਿ ਕਾਲਿ ਜੋ ਲੜਿਕੇ ਸਿਮਰੈ ਐਸੀ ਚਿੰਤਾ ਮਹਿ ਜੇ ਮਰੈ ॥

At the very last moment, one who thinks of his children, and dies in such thoughts,

ਸੂਕਰ ਜੋਨਿ ਵਲਿ ਵਲਿ ਅਉਤਰੈ ॥੩॥

shall be reincarnated over and over again as a pig. ||3||

ਅੰਤਿ ਕਾਲਿ ਜੋ ਮੰਦਰ ਸਿਮਰੈ ਐਸੀ ਚਿੰਤਾ ਮਹਿ ਜੇ ਮਰੈ ॥

At the very last moment, one who thinks of mansions, and dies in such thoughts,

ਪ੍ਰੇਤ ਜੋਨਿ ਵਲਿ ਵਲਿ ਅਉਤਰੈ ॥੪॥

shall be reincarnated over and over again as a goblin. ||4||

ਅੰਤਿ ਕਾਲਿ ਨਾਰਾਇਣੁ ਸਿਮਰੈ ਐਸੀ ਚਿੰਤਾ ਮਹਿ ਜੇ ਮਰੈ ॥

At the very last moment, one who thinks of the Lord, and dies in such thoughts,

ਬਦਤਿ ਤਿਲੋਚਨੁ ਤੇ ਨਰ ਮੁਕਤਾ ਪੀਤੰਬਰੁ ਵਾ ਕੇ ਰਿਦੈ ਬਸੈ ॥੫॥੨॥

says Trilochan, that man shall be liberated; the Lord shall abide in his heart. ||5||2||

— Sri Guru Granth Sahib, Ang 526

What happened to the 8.4 million cycle now? Here it is skipped, and the unfortunate soul is constantly reincarnated as the relevant creature. However, a prostitute is still a human, perhaps they could still have a chance? But the serpents and pigs are damned, how can they escape from their situation now? The problem here is not of contradiction but of both literalism on the behalf of the reader and a misunderstanding of the Guru's strategy.

The Guru employs these concepts as a technique to help progress to deeper understanding. Both these Shabads would be more or less relevant to different audiences, primarily those on the competency of karma. It is understandable and provides a set of necessary incentives for them to behave in a certain way. As they progress this concept can be less relied upon and new understanding can develop. Essentially, at later stages it is realised that it is God reincarnating themselves. When the body dies and disintegrates, that matter which once made up a "you", would go on to make up the soil, plants and animals. Reincarnation can then be seen as a great recycling of energy from one form to the next. When the atoms arrange themselves in a complex enough way, then the capacity to receive consciousness arises once again[4], and the "soul" re-emerges. This process is not just limited to after death either since the body is constantly undergoing decay and rejuvenation. Almost every cell in the body is replaced multiple times throughout the course of one's life. The skeleton replaces itself every ten years, red blood cells every four months and the skin between two to four weeks. The human being at birth is completely different to the one at death. To even call this a human *being* is misleading as it suggests a static entity. Perhaps a more accurate term is human *process*. Not even the mind is safe, as it constantly changes its ideas and beliefs. Memories themselves can be updated, manipulated and distorted or simply forgotten. When asking the question what happens after death, first we need to establish what exactly is it that is dying? This does not mean that reincarnation or karma etc. is not true. These are simply concepts more relevant at a particular level of understanding.

Why is any of this important? How does it relate to the topic of this manifesto? It is because...

You can't mix perspectives.

What is meant by this is that it is inconsistent to take conclusions from one level in order to operate at another level. For example, if we reject free-will but maintain a separate sense of self, then how can blame be placed on criminals? In fact, the entire justice system falls apart since no one is truly at fault. Even saying that previous sentence is false since there isn't any one individual in the first place to take the blame. The duality between good and evil also breaks down at higher competencies since it is all just God. Murder fails to be an ethical problem since God is the one killing and the one being killed. Yet very few will argue not to punish or remove murderers in society. Why? Because as long as we maintain a separate ego, we also attach to it the ability to differentiate and label our surroundings in terms of good/bad, hot/cold, high/low and more. Whereas objectively these things cannot exist without an observer or reference point from which to compare against. What is cold for a polar bear is different to what is cold for a camel. These dualities exist only in subjectivity. As long as there are individual subjects, then this is the realm of Karma and perhaps Upashana. These dualities can only exist at these levels. The only exception is that it begins to breakdown in Upashana, as what would otherwise be deemed inappropriate or unethical would be seen as necessary to the devotee. For example, the worship of stones, or seeing God as a singular rock would be shunned today, yet one of the contributors of Guru Granth Sahib, Bhagat Dhunna, did exactly this[5]. As someone on the competency of Upashana, they were carried through to achieve Brahmgyaan.

One of the primary positions that this manifesto is based upon is the right to *private property*. This a term to denote individual ownership over material items in the world. This includes houses, food, water, land, tools and even one's own body. However, if perspectives are mixed up, then a conflict seems to arise between Sikh philosophy and private property rights. It could be easily argued that "all things belong to God, therefore we cannot own anything" or "there is no self, so God must then own all things". Whilst this is implicitly true, it is only true in a relevant sense at a competency of wisdom. If this position is taken, then ethics (right and wrong) must also be rejected. Reincarnation, karma, heaven, hell, good, bad should all also be done away with. A separate sense of self cannot be rejected whilst also maintaining ethics or other relevant concepts. If a self is denied, then it must be consistently denied. Otherwise, whilst we are operating at competencies below Gyaan, then we must accept the right to property. How that property should be managed and organised is the very topic of this manifesto.

Therefore, Azadism is a philosophy concerned with the realm of Karma first, in order to build the foundations and provide the necessary conditions for those individuals looking to go further whilst protecting those who are at the very base Karmic level. It is not "wrong" or "bad" to own things, this is merely an attribute appropriate at these levels of understanding. It is from the perspective of Karam that the ideas in the manifesto are built up from - bottom up, not top down, since this is what the Guru does. They account for all levels, not just those already enlightened. This approach will be further reiterated in the first section, which will explore the implications of private property.

Further to the point, at the competency of Karam, where there still is an ego, to have ownership of property is appropriate just as much as it is to call a tyrant a tyrant and a saint a saint. At that level, all these labels can and do exist. Albeit illusory but even an illusion holds an existence. Recognise that these are just perspectives and each one does not exist in a vacuum. Observe the following picture:

From one perspective it is a rabbit, at another it is a duck. But both perspectives share a fundamental characteristic that there is indeed a picture there. The "somethingness" present is undeniable, it is just a difference in view and interpretation of that somethingness. Additionally, those views only exist so long as there is a viewer to interpret it. From the Karmic lens a duck or rabbit can be seen, whereas an Upashik says both rabbit or duck is something ("Prabhu, these are both you"). From the competency of Gyan neither distinction is recognised and only somethingness beyond any label or judgement is considered. This does not mean there is no duck, or rabbit, it just means that either is only seen so long as there is a separate individual available to interact and interpret it. Again, this is the perspective from which this manifesto will approach reality from for the sake of action.

Realising this distinction is not only crucial before beginning reading this manifesto, but also approaching spirituality in general. Bhai Gurdas Ji in his Vaaran warns of the dangers of mixing perspectives like this when criticising the misapplication of the Vedantic school of thought:

ਸਿਆਮ ਵੇਦ ਕਉ ਸੋਧਿ ਕਰਿ ਮਥਿ ਵੇਦਾਂਤੁ ਬਿਆਸਿ ਸੁਣਾਇਆ।

After studying/revising the Samaveda, Vyas (Badarayan) revealed/recited (the philosophy of) Vedanta

ਕਥਨੀ ਬਦਨੀ ਬਾਹਰਾ ਆਪੇ ਅਪਣਾ ਬ੍ਰਹਮੁ ਜਣਾਇਆ।

In his sermons he recognised himself as Brahm

ਨਦਰੀ ਕਿਸੈ ਨ ਲਿਆਵਈ ਹਉਮੈ ਅੰਦਰਿ ਭਰਮਿ ਭੁਲਾਇਆ।

No one can see Brahm, in Haumai and under illusion Brahm was forgotten

ਆਪੁ ਪੁਜਾਇ ਜਗਤ ਵਿਚਿ ਭਾਉ ਭਗਤਿ ਦਾ ਮਰਮੁ ਨ ਪਾਇਆ।

He placed himself as worthy of worship in the world, he did not recognise the importance of loving
devotion

ਤ੍ਰਿਪਤਿ ਨ ਆਵੀ ਵੇਦ ਮਥਿ ਅਗਨੀ ਅੰਦਰਿ ਤਪਤਿ ਤਪਾਇਆ।

Churning of the Vedas could not obtain peace for him and he started scorching one and all in the heat of
his ego.

ਮਾਇਆ ਡੰਡ ਨ ਉਤਰੇ ਜਮ ਡੰਡ ਬਹੁ ਦੁਖਿ ਰੁਆਇਆ।

When Maya's and the Yamraj's stick came down on him, he suffered greatly

ਨਾਰਦ ਮੁਨਿ ਉਪਦੇਸਿਆ ਮਥਿ ਭਾਗਵਤ ਗੁਨਿ ਗੀਤ ਕਰਾਇਆ।

After getting teachings from Narada, he recited and sang the praises of Bhagvat's (God) qualities.

ਬਿਨੁ ਸਰਨੀ ਨਹਿ ਕੋਇ ਤਰਾਇਆ ॥੧੧॥

Without the shade/protection (of the Guru), no one can get across (the world ocean)

— Bhai Gurdas Ji Vaaran, Vaar 1 Pauri 11: Vedant

The problem Bhai Ji is talking about is giving a teaching to someone who is not ready, that they are God themselves. However, if they do not successfully also understand that there is nothing but God, then this leads to a dangerous conclusion. Yes, they are God, but so is everyone else. They are only God because there is nothing left of themselves. God is that fundamental reality that is reached when removing all the illusory properties mapped on top of existence, such as an individual's desires, hates, beliefs, and even their own identity.

— Sri Guru Granth Sahib, Ang 736

Vedanta itself is made up of three approaches of Dvaita (dualistic) Vedanta, Advaita (non-dualistic) Vedanta and Vishistadvaita Vedanta (qualified non-duality) from which Bhagat Namdev, Bhagat Kabir and their Guru, Ramanand (who also has Shabads in Gurbani) descend from. The school of Advaita Vedanta are aware of the danger Bhai Gurdas mentions with their philosophy and so split their world view similarly into two parts[6], namely:

Paramarthika - Supreme/Ultimate
Vyavaharikha - Transactional

Whilst Paramarthika could be considered equal to the competency of Gyan, whereas everyday transactional reality is dealing in Maya, or the illusory reality that exists in duality. This dualistic perspective is where this manifesto sits, since it simply has to. Any discussion involving the role of justice systems implies ethics. Similarly assessing human behaviour and decision making on an individualist level implies separate selves. This is not a problem, the Guru themselves operated at these levels constantly throughout their lives, otherwise how would they have fought battles if they made arguments which confused perspectives? Instead they realised those levels, experienced it and took relevant teachings from it. For example, understanding that God is the supreme reality means that it is illogical to hold any deep hatred for another, since all are just acting out their role in this play of matter and energy. This is why the Guru can be understood to be Nirbhau Nirvair, since an enlightened being cannot physically hold fear or hatred without creating a duality. Whilst they recognised that it was God themselves swinging their Tulwar and decapitating the enemies on the battlefield, it still did not stop them engaging on the transactional plane. Even to help their Sikhs on this path, they come down to each Sikh on their level to lift them up and progress them spiritually. Azadism recognises this as it is simply a tool or set of ideas to be employed entirely on the transactional level. For those interested in Bhagti and advancing their level of competency, this manifesto is not appropriate. It is not aiming to do that, its purpose is different. If the reader is seeking that then read Gurbani and commit to doing Naam Abhiaas.

Therefore, in preparation for the rest of this manifesto, Azadism assumes free-will and private property as a necessary first step. This allows for law and order to be established on a system of ethics and grants individuals sovereignty over their own lives, as well as the ability to choose how they live it, free from oppression and tyranny. The first section will discuss other assumptions built upon this.

Private property as a premise will not be mentioned further after this introduction, but it is something the reader may want to keep in mind as a backdrop to later concepts mentioned in this manifesto as necessary pre-requisite in understanding. For example, when discussing tyranny, an inherent understanding that a tyrant destroys the right to private property when they kill or steal from others should be obvious. However, if the reader approaches this from a Gyanic or Paramatmic perspective, then there is no tyrant nor oppressed. Therefore, for the purpose of this manifesto, private property is a necessary assumption. Even to give in charity requires it, since if you own nothing, then how can you give anything away? Whilst it is ultimately true that it is simply God giving and taking themselves, for the purpose of this manifesto the author suggests putting this mindset aside for the time being. The same way the Guru sent away his court philosophers and theologians in the time of war, this manifesto makes a similar suggestion. The reason the Guru did this was because for battle a particular state of mind and readiness to act is required, whereas those fixated on ethics would debate the Guru on every step taken. There is a Sama for everything. Only by letting private ownership over one's possessions and one's own body and mind can you have something to work up from. Trying to limit all action based on the concept of oneness is a ridiculous strategy to develop anything. The Guru could have easily just written Ik and been done. They understood the nature of human beings and broke it down. Oankaar is the first breakdown of Ik into three states of waking, dreaming, dreamless sleep, and the fourth state of Turiya[7]. The rest of Mool Mantar expounds on this before further expansion through Japu Ji Sahib and the rest the Sri Guru Granth Sahib. At the very least, let there be a reasonable starting point. Then by your own choice, you can give up your own private property through charity all you like. But enforcing that on everyone is the root of immorality. This is no way to progress through these stages.

Those higher states can be written about forever, however the only way of truly understanding it is experiencing it for oneself. The explanation of these things becomes very intricate and difficult, and will fall too much outside of the scope of this manifesto. I have only given enough here to drive the point about being careful of mixing perspectives, since the last thing a reader needs is to approach these economic ideas with confused world-views. Again, it must be repeatedly stressed that this topic needs careful attention not to confuse perspectives. Even writing the above few paragraphs were perhaps the hardest to write in this entire manifesto. As the author, I had to be very cautious here since people could easily take it the wrong way. In writing this, many of the sentences had to be rewritten to account for this. Guru Nanak's description of talking about these things is truly appropriate:

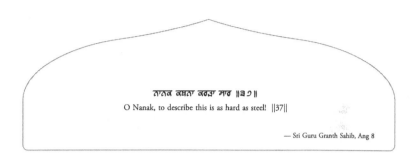

ਨਾਨਕ ਕਥਨਾ ਕਰੜਾ ਸਾਰ ॥੩੭॥

O Nanak, to describe this is as hard as steel! ||37||

— Sri Guru Granth Sahib, Ang 8

With this understanding in mind, we will now discuss the topic of this manifesto.

Miri

ਰਾਜਨੀਤੀ ਦੀ ਪੜ੍ਹਾਈ

Study politcs

— Sri Guru Gobind Singh, Hukam 28

The 28th command from the Guru to his Khalsa encourages us to study the art of statecraft and politics. However, discussion of this topic within the Panth often misses a crucial element to nation building that forms the very bedrock of determining the success of a people. This crucial component is the field of *economics*.

Economics is often reduced to the study of wealth and money management of a nation, however this often misses the more fundamental questions it seeks to address. It is an inquiry into the study of human behaviour itself. Economics looks at incentives that drive human beings, it seeks to understand why we make certain choices over others. Money is an inseparable part of life whether we like it or not. Therefore, economics is often conflated with monetary matters since money drives so much of our decision making. Through money we trade, offer gifts, command labour and attain power. Money is not just the paper notes or metal coins, it is a symbol representing *value*. Through exchanging value we sustain what is known as the economy. What one person values more is obtained by giving up something they value less. But how this is managed in a society is pivotal for its development and more critically, its survival. Without a functioning economy empires collapse, people starve and hell manifests on earth. The worst atrocities imaginable occur when basic needs can no longer be met. Understanding economics allows us to avoid these catastrophes and answer questions such as: how best to remove poverty? Why are some nations richer than others? What environments allow for maximum innovation?

How should a government be structured to ensure the human rights of all can be protected?

On an individual level, the study of economics can be invaluable in building and securing wealth. Recognising how money works and how different types of policy can increase or decrease prosperity can help navigate one to financial and political success. Understanding the inflationary nature of the money supply and decrease in purchasing power leads to an appreciation of the value of investing rather than just saving. Becoming cognizant of how to play this game can grant financial freedom, allowing people to change focus from simply chasing money to letting it chase them, thereby allowing time to concentrate on more meaningful endeavours in life. As well as the potential financial benefits, the psychological aspects are perhaps even more important. Through adopting an investor mindset, a higher time preference is achieved where an individual is willing to forgo pleasure now in order to reap a bigger reward later. This helps develop a necessary long-term mindset that the Panth seems to be lacking especially. By permeating the study of Economics, we are able to transition from a community that is reactive and responds only when there is an imminent threat or a tragedy (even this is ineffective most of the time), to one that is proactive and already has the necessary systems in place to both avoid and mitigate the harmful effects of such events[8]. As well as this, not only does studying economics allow us to meet the above mandate from our Guru, but for the Khalsa this study allows us to better understand the world around us in order to avoid manipulation and exploitation. One of the most recent examples of this being the Kisaan Morcha in India[9]. Additionally, learning how economics really works may help Sikhs save themselves from both external and internal threats.

On observation, there has been a rise in certain ideas within the Panth that seem to not only go against basic principles of economics, but are also antithetical to Sikhi itself. Alongside much of the population, we Sikhs are increasingly falling prey to misinformation and ignorance. Petty squabbles about largely meaningless things have become the norm, and society all around us is becoming more and more polarised in terms of left-wing and right-wing nonsense. But this is a distraction. The real problem is, and has always been, the battle between liberty and authoritarianism. Therefore, this manifesto is an attempt to combat these bad ideas, with a set of better ideas drawing from both Sikh principles and the latest developments in the field of economics. Azadism combines these two aspects into an ideology that prioritises the same freedom that our Gurus and Shaheeds fought and attained martyrdom for.

The reality is this - not only are their nations that hold power and influence that the Khalsa should have already had at this point, but even single individuals have more power than perhaps the entire Panth combined. The worst part is that these people abuse their power to oppress, murder and steal, and the Khalsa has no current way of stopping or replacing them. It may be argued that nothing will beat the Guru's Khalsa, and whilst true, this has not been seen to prevent the otherwise avoidable genocides and brutal oppression of today. We are so behind on the global level for these things, and as result needless and preventable suffering goes unchecked. It is time for a rethinking in our approach. A realignment of our goals and objectives so that Guru Khalsa Panth is able to navigate the complexity of the modern world and avoid propaganda and misinformation. But to do so, we must accurately define the problem. We must learn from history - both the successes and the failures. Knowledge is a tool that can be used both against us and for us. Acquiring knowledge ourselves is a necessary means of defence in this age of information warfare.

The manifesto will begin on the topic of self-interest and the power of incentives in both spiritual and economic decision-making. It is important that this chapter is read carefully since it provides the foundations for the rest of sections to build upon. The second section will introduce the concepts of markets, and the economic laws of supply and demand. After that, the topic of privatisation will be explored through the concepts of competition and monopolies. This section will also outline two key examples of how industries would function under an Azadist framework. From there, methods in which to support people in an economy will be discussed, as well as taxes and inequality. The final section outlines the role of a government and presents an idea in how the principles of an Azadist economy can be preserved. The reader is strongly encouraged to consult the corresponding notes for each section, since many extra aspects that were not included in the main body is present there. The notes also show the sources and relevant information to help solidify your understanding or delve into more detail about certain topics.

The goal of this manifesto is to open a gateway in understanding to a world of thinking that every Khalsa needs to become aware of. We should abandon this game of trying to play catch up with the "West" and look towards getting ahead. The world is changing at a rapid rate, and our attachment to old ways will keep us trailing behind. Simply mimicking the past is useless without understanding its lessons. What use is to dress up as a warrior and amass a great collection of mediaeval weapons if they will never be used? This is not saying to abandon appearances or practices, it is an encouragement to live up to them. By uncovering key principles a new approach must be taken that is applicable to today. The Gurus did not stick to just swords and bows, they themselves developed their own cannons, used firearms, gathered world-class poets, musicians and philosophers of the day, all to present the principles of their message in the most relevant way. The Guru's Darbar being a prime example for the Khalsa, as an institution that facilitated the flourishing of art, philosophy and science. Similarly today, our Panth must recognise the importance of getting to the top of cutting edge fields such as: economics, finance, politics, psychology, philosophy, natural sciences, mathematics, machine learning, artificial intelligence, blockchains and cryptocurrencies. The Khalsa should be permeated throughout these areas, but where are our world class institutions, universities and industry leaders? The excuse that we are so few of the population is not acceptable. We have had far less numbers and endured far worse suffering in our history. The problem isn't numbers, it is how we use them.

Inevitably, there will be those who are stuck in their thinking and are unwilling to adapt. This manifesto is not trying to convince them. The aim here is only to convey a set of ideas to those within the Panth that are actually genuine about doing Khoj and taking the mandates of our Guru seriously, such as the one above. Neither is this manifesto aiming to be an economics textbook. Taking inspiration from Thomas Sowell's book, *Basic Economics*[10], you will find no complicated graphs nor mathematical notation, save from the few simple diagrams and tables designed to help visualise a concept clearly. Additionally, particular inspiration has been taken from the

Austrian School of Economics as a resource for many of the economic ideas present in this manifesto[11].

An important disclaimer

Firstly, the reader needs to ensure the utmost respect is given when handling this manifesto since it contains Gurbani. For this reason, a paper copy is only provided upon request and collected or delivered in person. For more information, please see the website. Otherwise the full manifesto is available on the website for free and also in PDF format. The Sangat is encouraged to download and secure copies on their hard drives to avoid potential future loss of data for any reason on the author's behalf. Secondly, not all Panktis will have an accompanying interpretation. The reason being that the same Gurbani may resonate differently based on a person's own individual spiritual level, and so to force an interpretation for each line is unnecessary. The reader is therefore encouraged to use the selected Shabads as a start point for their own Vichaar, and the responsibility is on them to do further Khoj. This doesn't have to be done alone, and you can even contact me to discuss your interpretations of these lines (or anything discussed here). I have included Shabads as a support item for the themes talked about in this manifesto, as a sort of start point for your own Khoj and as a suggestion on what to contemplate. But again, the responsibility is your own. Only when you yourself take the responsibility to do your own Vichaar, and apply it to your own lives will you get an interpretation appropriate for you. SriGranth and SikhiToTheMax have both been invaluable resources in accessing these Shabads, and on there you are able to study translations in English and Punjabi, alongside interpretations from the Faridkot Teeka. These are not just throwing random Panktis at you, time has been spent on selecting these. But they have been limited to only a few on purpose. Use them as a springboard for your own Vichaar and do not hesitate to bring your Vichaar to me to discuss. Any disagreements are also encouraged, and you are more than welcome to present your counter-arguments.

The entirety of this manifesto is the author's own views and interpretations of both Sikhi and economics. The positions taken on subjects in this document does not intend to be presented as objective fact. The only position that is fixed is that there is precisely no one universal understanding of any of these things. Just like Prachin Panth Prakash is a unique view of Rattan Singh Bhangu's Sikhi, or Suraj Prakash is an expression of Kavi Santokh Singh's Sikhi (especially his Prem for the Gurus), any text related to Sikhi outside of Gurbani (including this one) is the author's own subjective take on it. This is merely one application of Sikhi on the study of economics. There is no objective interpretation on purpose due to the strategy of the Guru in disseminating Sikhi mentioned earlier.

What is presented here is what the author believes is the most accurate reconciliation between economic ideas and Sikh principles. If there are any disagreements then please feel free to get in touch to debate or discuss any of this. This work is an homage to the vast collection of knowledge studied in Sri Guru Gobind Singh's Darbars. Mahraj themselves encouraged the study and translation of texts not limited to just spirituality, but also in subjects like statecraft, sciences, health and medicine, poetry, musical theory etc. Similarly, most of the ideas in this manifesto are already in existence. All the author is aiming to do is to bring these concepts into the Panth and relate it directly to Sikhi for the benefit of the Khalsa and the Sangat, and in turn to benefit all humanity. The author hopes this work inspires others to do the same with topics such as law, finance, politics, but also modern science and medicine, quantum physics, artificial intelligence, blockchains, or even poetry and art (although there is a lot of existing talent here already).

Since the author of this manifesto is most definitely fallible, there is bound to be mistakes or other views that could fit better with Sikhi. It is for this reason debate and discourse here is repeatedly encouraged in order to assess which ideas are indeed more or less relevant. In fact this manifesto itself is a counter-argument for certain pro-central planning ideas that have grown in popularity within the Panth that in the author's opinion are not only foreign to Sikhi but also destructive to it.

Outside of the main body of this text, please also refer to the relevant Notes for each section. A glossary of terms has also been provided, alongside an appendix. Additionally, consult the website for updates and future posts and publications.

Through this manifesto, the aim is that the door becomes opened for debate and discussion on these topics, and an effort to educate ourselves on some of the most important ideas of today. The Khalsa was made manifest to free people from Ghulami, not become it ourselves.

ਹਉਮੈ ਦੀਰਘ ਰੋਗੁ ਹੈ ਦਾਰੂ ਭੀ ਇਸੁ ਮਾਹਿ ॥

Ego is a chronic disease, but it contains its own cure as well.

I
Self-Interest

Forming the foundations of an Azadist society.

Azadism works off the assumption that people generally act according to their own self-interest. For the vast majority, the motivations behind one's actions is how the consequences of those actions will benefit them first. Many may disguise this as working for the best interest of others such as family, friends, or community, but even this can be argued to arise from an inherent desire to appease their own self-interest. Consider those cases of politicians or celebrities helping with charity work, are they really doing it to solve the issues or to increase their own reputations? Only they know their own intent. Now this does not mean that there is no place for Seva, but it should be made clear that only that type of service that is done out of selflessness and with no desire for reward can be truly considered a true spiritual effort[1].

ਸੇਵਾ ਕਰਤ ਹੋਇ ਨਿਹਕਾਮੀ ॥

One who performs selfless service, without thought of reward

ਤਿਸ ਕਉ ਹੋਤ ਪਰਾਪਤਿ ਸੁਆਮੀ ॥

Shall attain his Lord and Master.

— Sri Guru Granth Sahib, Ang 286

It can be argued that only when one has reached this state of mind, are they doing a "selfless" Seva in the true sense, whereby, there is a merger between their own self-interest and the self-interest of others. This could even be considered as the destruction of self-interest entirely. For someone who recognises God in everyone and everything (including themselves), what "self" is left for them to act in their own interest? This is the goal of spiritual pursuit - the successful denial of duality and recognition of absolute oneness[2].

ਕਬੀਰ ਤੂੰ ਤੂੰ ਕਰਤਾ ਤੂ ਹੂਆ ਮੁਝ ਮਹਿ ਰਹਾ ਨ ਹੂੰ ॥

Kabeer, repeating, ""You, You"", I have become like You. Nothing of me remains in myself.

ਜਬ ਆਪਾ ਪਰ ਕਾ ਮਿਟਿ ਗਇਆ ਜਤ ਦੇਖਉ ਤਤ ਤੂ ॥੨੦੪॥

When the difference between myself and others is removed, then wherever I look, I see only You. ||204||

— Sri Guru Granth Sahib, Ang 1375

However, it is unreasonable to assume that everyone is by default at this level. An Azadist system takes into consideration a population that is at all levels of spiritual attainment, by working bottom up. It recognises that Seva in the true sense is done only by a minority of people and the majority work often out of a self-interest motive. Azadism builds off the premise that until someone is at that stage and remains so, they are usually acting out in a way that best maximises the benefit to themselves first and foremost. This is not a necessarily a bad thing, it is reasonable to argue that the Guru themselves realised the importance of this. This can be shown through the many examples of them appealing to people's self-interest in order to promote engagement with the spiritual process. In effect, they suggest that following the principles of Sikhi *is* in the person's best interest. There are many reoccurring themes throughout Gurbani following a template of presenting an ideal or recommending a certain behaviour, and then offering and explaining the reward of doing so[3, 4, 5].

ਜਉ ਸੁਖ ਕਉ ਚਾਹੈ ਸਦਾ ਸਰਨਿ ਰਾਮ ਕੀ ਲੇਹ ॥

If you yearn for eternal peace, then seek the Sanctuary of the Lord.

ਕਹੁ ਨਾਨਕ ਸੁਨਿ ਰੇ ਮਨਾ ਦੁਰਲਭ ਮਾਨੁਖ ਦੇਹ ॥੨੭॥

Says Nanak, listen, mind: this human body is difficult to obtain. ||27||

— Sri Guru Granth Sahib, Ang 1427

ਸਤਿਗੁਰ ਸੇਵਾ ਸਫਲ ਹੈ ਬਣੀ ॥

Service to the True Guru is fruitful and rewarding;

ਜਿਤੁ ਮਿਲਿ ਹਰਿ ਨਾਮੁ ਧਿਆਇਆ ਹਰਿ ਧਣੀ ॥

meeting Him, I meditate on the Name of the Lord, the Lord Master.

ਜਿਨ ਹਰਿ ਜਪਿਆ ਤਿਨ ਪੀਛੈ ਛੂਟੀ ਘਣੀ ॥੧॥

So many are emancipated along with those who meditate on the Lord. ||1||

— Sri Guru Granth Sahib, Ang 165

ਸਮਰ ਸਾਮੁਹੇ ਸੀਸ ਤੋ ਪੈ ਚੜ੍ਹਾਵੈ ॥ ਮਹਾਂ ਭੂਪ ਹ੍ਵੈ ਅੰਤਰਿ ਰਾਜ ਪਾਵੈ ॥

[The one] who, in war, places his head before You. [They shall become] a great King and in the next life
will attain a Kingdom as well.

ਮਹਾਂ ਭਾਵ ਸੋਂ ਜੋ ਕਰੈ ਤੋਰ ਪੂਜਾ ॥ ਸਮਰ ਜੀਤ ਕੈ ਸੁਰ ਹ੍ਵੈ ਹੈ ਅਦੂਜਾ ॥

With great love those who worship You ! Those warriors achieve victory on the battle field and get
liberated !

ਤੁਮੈ ਪੂਜਹੀਂ ਬੀਰ ਬਾਨੈਤ ਭਾਰੀ ॥ ਮਹਾਂ ਖੜਗਧਾਰੀ ਮਹਾਂ ਤੇਜ ਅਰੀ ॥

The Great Kshtriya warriors, in their uniform, worship you. [You are] the Great Sword-bearer and the
ferocious Shastradhari [weapon-bearer] Warrior !

ਪੜੈ ਪ੍ਰੀਤਿ ਸੋਂ ਪ੍ਰਾਤ ਅਸਟੋਤ੍ਰ ਜਾ ਕੋ ॥ ਕਰੈ ਰੁਦ੍ਰ ਕਾਲੀ ਨਮਸਕਾਰ ਤਾ ਕੋ ॥

Whosoever repeats this Astotar (with love) in the early morning, Rudra [Shiv Ji] and Kali both salute you !

— Sri Dassam Bani, Bhagouti Astotar

The specific interpretations of these Shabads is not what is being brought
attention to here. Instead, observe the way the Shabad has been constructed
to deliver an Updesh; the way a formula is followed of providing the listener
or reader with *incentives*. Further to this, the Guru also provides Shabads
warning Sikhs of the consequences of not behaving in accordance with their
teachings too[6].

We can also look at the history of Guru Gobind Singh Ji and how he used
financial incentives specifically to promote certain behaviours. We can look
at his Darbar compromising of world-class poets, Raagis and philosophers,
and how the Guru used to offer cash prizes as rewards for displays of
excellence[7]. Another example is the armies of the Guru who were paid
regular wages as a reward for their service. This all appeals to the self-
interest of the Sikhs at the time. The Guru would have recognised and
accepted the fact that not all his Sikhs were completely selfless Sant
Mahapurash, who had already successfully destroyed any sense of desire and
were fully merged with the one. Hence, their very purpose was to lead the
people to reach those states of enlightenment. It is far more reasonable to
accept that people are at different levels of spiritual development, and so the
Guru takes this into account and crafts techniques that will work for all, not

just those already on higher levels of consciousness. This approach is clarified by Guru Arjan Dev themselves in a Sakhi from Bhai Mani Singh's *Sikhan Di Bhagat Mala*, where the Guru outlines the three levels of people's understanding. He caters for this by providing Shabads that vary in degrees of relevancy depending on someone's level of competency[8]. Ultimately, the pursuit of these things leads to an understanding that doing Simran and Seva are in themselves their own rewards, but this may take time and effort to realise. To get someone to realise this, an incentive is a perfectly reasonable way to get them started. In the same way, a doctor may explain the benefits of a medicine to an ill person, the Guru explains the benefits of Naam to all humanity. However, as the aforementioned Sakhi shows us, the Guru recognises the various illnesses specific to each individual and so provides the relevant medicine for every case. Hence why the Guru is *Jagat Guru*.

Taking these factors into consideration, the population of an Azadist nation is similarly not assumed to be already enlightened. Azadism provides a system in which every individual is accounted for based on their own personal level of spiritual attainment, ranging from Malechh to Mahapurakh. Under this system, even those pursuing self-interest alone, will still benefit everyone else in the process (given a certain condition which will be explained later).

> *"It is not from the benevolence of the butcher, the brewer, or the baker that we expect our dinner, but from their regard to their own self-interest. We address ourselves not to their humanity but to their self-love, and never talk to them of our own necessities, but of their advantages"*

— *Adam Smith, The Wealth Of Nations, Book I, Chapter II*

The above quote by late eighteenth-century political philosopher, Adam Smith (considered the father of economics), tells us that the butcher does not supply his services because he necessarily has an innate selflessness. He does this expecting to be compensated with something in return that satisfies his effort and his desire for a reward. The fact that others also benefit from this transaction is only a by-product of the butcher's self-interest orientated behaviour. The butcher may or may not value the health and well-being of others' families more than his own, only he himself truly knows. However, let's assume that the butcher is greedy and only wants to create enough wealth for him and his family, but to do so, he must provide a good or service that others are willing to pay for. He can only satisfy his 'needs and wants' by satisfying the 'needs and wants' of others.

This does not mean that we must always strive to act out in self-interest. But, considering the fact we cannot guarantee everyone will always be compassionate, the best course of action is to maintain such a system that embeds positive outcomes regardless of intent at a base level to work up from. In the process this mitigates the perceivably harmful effect of those who are greedy, so that by them pursuing greed, the best interests of others are not compromised. It must be clarified that greed is not simply the equivalent of self-interest, but rather an *excess* of it.

Whilst it is widely accepted that as per Sikhi, greed is a vice that should be avoided, a government cannot set ethics without the threat of force, and so Azadism argues that it should not as a result. If a government has the power to set ethics, then it is more susceptible to oppress its people to conform to the subjective beliefs of whatever ethical framework the government in power dictates. It will then also use this as an excuse to commit atrocities to uphold the chosen "ideal" it wishes to advocate. We need to only look at history to see this: Hitler made it "unethical" to be a Jew, the Chinese Communist Party is doing the same with the Uyghurs right now, and in our own history, Indira Gandhi made it immoral to be Sikh. Obviously, this was disguised in different ways such as saying the Jews are greedy, or Sikhs are terrorists, but fundamentally this is the extremes of what could happen and has happened, when government is given the monopoly on ethic setting. It is for this reason that, although greed is a vice according to Sikhi, the means in which to remove it should never be handed over to the state to enforce through violence.

The government is the one entity that we should actively ensure does not act in its own self-interest, since it has the "legal" power to enforce it more than any other entity. How then does one eliminate the self-interest motive or greed? As touched upon earlier, this can only ever be truly achieved through spiritual pursuit. Whilst there could be a selection process for government officials that considers spiritual attainment, the other option is to reduce the power and size of the government in the first place to mitigate the risks. By having a government that has influence over fewer things, then in the case it degenerates into immorality it won't have such a widespread effect over its people. The exact checks and balances that could be installed will be expanded upon in the last section.

> *Every individual... neither intends to promote the*
> *public interest, nor knows how much he is*
> *promoting it... he intends only his own security;*
> *and by directing that industry in such a manner as*
> *its produce may be of the greatest value, he intends*
> *only his own gain, and he is in this, as in many*
> *other cases, led by an invisible hand to promote an*
> *end which was no part of his intention.*

— *Adam Smith, The Wealth Of Nations, Book IV, Chapter II*

Self-interest forms the base of an Azadist society. It is through this that trade can occur, where two or more parties can reach an agreement for exchange in which each party considers their own self-interest. If something is not mutually beneficial, then that transaction would not occur. What someone considers as beneficial for them is completely subjective, as everyone will have their own unique needs and wants to satisfy. Even this varies as the increased consumption of a particular good may reduce the desire or utility of an additional unit of that good. The market is a flurry of these transactions done out of self-interest; this is the reason why there is no need for any central planning. By only tending to their own needs, each individual satisfies the needs of society as a whole. No one part must understand the whole in order to make a decision, the same way a lion doesn't consult an ecologist before hunting its prey. Yet nature rebalances as required.

These concepts will be expanded upon in the next section, however where the line is drawn is when someone's self-interest negatively impacts the self-interest of others. For example, if someone subjectively finds it beneficial to them to pollute a river used by farmers for irrigation, then since this affects the farmer's own self-interest in being able to grow their crops to sell for a profit, or the consumers who will have to eat that food, the government's role is to step in and rectify the situation[9]. This introduces the main principle on which an Azadist nation must abide by and in which the rest of the system relies upon - the "non-aggression principle" (NAP). This is the idea that everyone is free to live however they want to, as long as it does not impede the right for others to do the same. The sole basis on which the government can act is to maintain the NAP. To rephrase this in terms of interest, it is the freedom to pursue one's own self-interest as long as it doesn't harm the right for others to do the same. It would be illegal under an Azadist government to force anyone to engage in a transaction they deny, and this is the government's responsibility to enforce this law. The above is a clear example of the NAP being broken, and this is where the government's role is realised. If self-interest is the sand and gravel, the NAP is the cement which forms the concrete foundations of an Azadist economy.

To reiterate, this system does not need to rely on the morality of its participants. However, just because the foundation includes self-interest, it does not mean that the rest of the structure must conform to this standard. There is ample room for spiritual pursuit, where people are more than free to sacrifice their own self-interest for the betterment of others. In fact, if what benefits someone the most is to increase the quality of life of others, an Azadist citizen is free to pursue how best to satisfy this legitimate interest as long as it does not violate the NAP. This can take the form of private charity, religious institutions, and civil society in general, as will be explored further in the fourth section. Therefore, Azadism is built from the bottom up in terms of ethics, meaning that instead of assuming everyone is already enlightened and altruistic, it channels greed in a way that even by pursuing it, society does not suffer. And those who abandon greed for compassion, then society naturally benefits from this also. The importance is stressed upon the freedom to choose, constrained only by a non-aggression principle.

To conclude this first section, a repeated emphasis must be placed on the power of incentives, as this will be touched upon throughout this manifesto. During the British Raj, the government sought to fix the problem of deadly cobras infesting Delhi. To solve this, they offered to pay anyone who brought them dead cobras. Whilst initially this seemed like a good idea to reduce the population of these snakes, what they had effectively done was create a market for dead snakes. Now people were breeding them to get a stable income from the government. The lesson from this story became known as the "Cobra Effect" and highlights the necessity in factoring in incentives in any sort of policy making[10].

II

Markets

Money, Trade and the Laws of Supply & Demand

Fundamentally, Azadism is based upon the free interactions between people, constantly exchanging with each other to satisfy needs and wants in a society. Azadism promotes a system in which people, acting out of their own self-interest (within a certain limit), can freely exchange goods and services to meet the societal requirements of production, consumption and distribution of wealth. Human beings are in a unique position in a variety of ways, and one of the early developments that was necessary to produce the level of success we as a species have had has been the ability to cooperate, compete and communicate. These traits culminated into a system in which we were able trade and barter for resources rather than having to just kill and steal in a constant struggle for survival.

Consider the example of early human tribes, whereby one tribesman becomes an expert in hunting and can acquire more meat than he is able to consume all by himself. However, due to his success his weapons constantly need repair or replacement. Another tribesman finds that he is better suited at repairing or making better quality weapons rather than hunt himself. The hunter recognises the potential for these and decides that in exchange for those weapons he will give him some of his extra food. The weapon maker needs the food, and the hunter needs the weapons. Or, in other words, the hunter values the weapons more than he values the extra food that he does not consume, and on the other side, the weapon maker values the food more than the weapons he cannot use as effectively as the hunter. By having a system of exchange, the hunter has another option instead of simply fighting with others and taking what they have. There is now an opportunity to cooperate. The hunter recognises a greater benefit in cooperating in this way as the superior quality weapons makes his hunting easier, and more fruitful. The weapon-maker, instead of having to go out hunting can devote his time to hone his craft and perhaps innovate further.

This example forms the basis of what is known as the *market*, which is run upon the subjective value each participant places on different goods and services. In time, this symbiotic relationship would develop as more people enter the market to exchange what they value less for something they value more. As this occurs different areas of specialisation develops, since more time is devoted in other areas of the survival process[1]. Now, not everyone has to be a hunter and instead may provide other goods or services to trade with the hunter for food. From this, even secondary markets can be developed to exchange more than just food. It became unnecessary for everyone to revolve their lives around finding their next meals like animals. People were now able to devote time to new ways of producing things that others valued and were willing to trade for. It is from this type of cooperation in a society in which tasks could be broken up into parts, and individuals could focus on delivering a part of the process rather than the whole. The hunter no longer needs to spread out his time to cover making weapons, hunting, and cooking. Through trade, these tasks could be handed over to others, freeing up time to focus on one in order to specialise and gradually build valuable experience and efficiency. With trade and markets, people become free to pursue and develop many other necessary crafts that have led to the innumerable innovations of the human race. Allowing the opportunity for people not to just focus on their base requirements and mere survival gave way for the formation of key institutions in our evolution as a race, including things such as agriculture, arts, religion and more.

Eventually, a common medium of exchange had to develop due to the following issues. Imagine a farmer who owns a large herd of cows, but owned no horses. From his point of view, he may value a horse being worth three of his cows, and so looks for a seller that will be willing to trade with him. When he enters a marketplace, he may realise that horse sellers generally would exchange for a different number of cows. The farmer will weigh up his options. If he finds a seller that is only asking for three or less cows then he is likely to trade otherwise if the price of a horse in terms of cows is more than this, he may not trade. However, what happens if horse sellers do not want cows but need bread instead? They could possibly buy and sell the cows in the hopes that a baker wants them, but then this poses another problem. A single cow may be worth 100 loaves of bread, but how many cows would exchange for a single loaf? Unless you cut the cow into parts and hope the bread maker wants that, this transaction would be unlikely to occur.

Therefore, over time money was introduced as a common object that everything in a market could be exchanged for. This has taken many forms throughout history, but most popularly it has been in the form of precious metals such as gold and silver. These could be subdivided or melted together easily into different weights representing different values. They could be carried around conveniently and also act as a store of wealth. A few ounces of gold could represent many cows, without having to take the entire herd with you to the marketplace. Instead of butchering the cow to buy bread, they could sell it for some silver, and maybe use a tenth of an ounce of it to get their loaf and know that it will be accepted. This is a key advantage of giving money the ability to determine prices more accurately. Through different weights of gold, you can calculate in terms of that gold, how many cows are worth one loaf of bread. Suppose one cow was worth a hundred ounces of silver and a loaf of bread was worth one ounce of silver. In effect, you are now able to sell a hundredth of a cow for a loaf without having to cut off parts of the cow. Over time, civilisations were able to standardise these weights to make exchange more accurate and trade easier. Later on, this was made even more easier by banks who could hold your physical gold in their secure vaults and issue you a paper note. This would represent a "promise" from the bank that you could redeem your gold at any time. This paper currency would be then used to transfer ownership of that gold in market interactions[2]. But what determines how much money can be traded for an amount of goods or services? How is the price of something calculated?

In a market, there will be many buyers and sellers with a variety of wants and needs to be met. Due to the self-interest motive, buyers aim to purchase at low prices and sellers are aiming to get the highest price. However, in a competitive market there are many options, and so a seller cannot just raise their prices excessively since buyers will just go to another seller. Similarly, a buyer couldn't offer to pay a price too far below what other buyers are willing to pay, since no one would sell to them when they know they can get a better deal. This conflict of interest between buyers and sellers allow for a natural, market price to be determined for goods and services. This is known as the the *supply and demand* of goods and services. Where the supplier produces a quantity of goods at a price meeting the amount demanded at that same level, this is known as the *equilibrium* price (the natural, market price).

It is important to recognise what the price is composed of, and perhaps more fundamentally, value itself. Traditionally this was usually thought of in terms of the costs incurred upon the supplier of a good or service in the production of them. Adam Smith in his 'Wealth of Nations' mentions some of these primary factors in determining prices as: the time and effort (labour) that went into it, the costs involved with purchasing or using materials, and/or the land required in the process. It also includes a profit which is the extra amount of money obtained in a sale beyond the costs that went into production[3]. This profit incentive is what tends to drive suppliers the most, since it is through this profit that they can go on to purchase other items in the market that they need. Why would anyone go through all this effort and take on the risk involved if they just break even or make a loss? There is a place for this in charity, but for the most part, people create something that is valued in society so that in return, they can get something that they value back[4].

Although the idea about the amount of labour put into the production of a good determines its price is relatively correct and is still a valid theory applicable to many goods and services, it does fail to account for all instances[5]. If the costs of the factors of production increase, then usually things that rely on those factors also raise in price. For instance, if the cost of metal rises for whatever reason, then the cost to produce a sword from that metal would also rise. This may then be reflected in the price the final customer must pay for that sword. Later however, certain limitations to this theory of value became apparent through economists such as Carl Menger, the founder of the Austrian School of Economics. Instead, he argued that the value of a good was determined by how useful it was to the buyer, not how much work went into producing it. The buyer generally doesn't care or even know in most circumstances. A diamond found in the dirt would sell for the same amount as one dug out after a thousand days of hard labour in a mine (given the same size and shape)[6]. As was touched upon in the previous section, even this perceived value on the buyer's side is not fixed. Someone stuck in a desert would value water far greater than someone living next to a river, and would therefore be willing to exchange far more in a trade for it than the latter person[7]. Another example would be umbrellas. An umbrella when it's raining is worth more than when it is not, despite the fact that the exact same labour went into producing it. Further to this, it is unlikely that an extra umbrella would be valued the same to you after the first one. The same way, gradually if you keep selling water to someone in a desert, after a certain point, each extra bottle would be worth less and less to them[8]. The same product is valued differently based on the subjective beliefs of the one purchasing it, which is affected by all sorts of circumstances. Some people are willing to pay more, and some less. The average price we tend to find on things is therefore the combined subjective values of everyone participating in the market.

Combining these ideas, a suitable answer arose to the infamous "diamond-water" paradox that had perplexed Adam Smith. This was the confusion as to why diamonds were worth more than water since water was far more important in sustaining life. Diamonds on the other hand have far less usefulness in comparison for survival. This is because, although water may be more important, it becomes less important to you the more you have it. Since water is not scarce like diamonds, it would naturally be valued less since you can easily satisfy your need for it. There is less to give up on your side in a trade for it. Diamonds on the other hand are far harder to come by, and so each additional unit of water is worth far less than each additional unit of diamond[9].

In the study of economics, *scarcity* is one of the initial concepts that is introduced, which is the reality that there is a limited amount of resources compared to an unlimited amount of wants and needs. Where a certain amount of resource is used up, it is in effect preventing those resources to be used elsewhere in a different way. What markets allow for is a system in which resources are allocated to wherever the people themselves deem relevant. If the demand for cars increase, then the supplier of cars make more since there is a higher rate of income available for the production of that good. If the resources to produce them begin to deplete and become harder to obtain, then the supplier has to raise prices. As prices rise, demand falls on the consumer side, since more people cannot afford it. They would value the money they have now more than what they can buy with it, and so either hold on to it or spend it elsewhere. Those who can still afford it are essentially signalling that their subjective value of that car still matches with the supplier's price for it. This then rebalances production levels to reduce the amount of resources used to make cars in order to meet this new reduced demand.

The self organising qualities of a market requires no central authority to determine how much or how little something should be produced. It will adapt depending on the scarcity. There is also no need for a central planner to decide what should and should not be produced, since whatever there is a demand for will be made available by those seeking a profit, and what people don't want or need won't be supplied. This is known as "price signalling", which is the market's own way of communicating where resources should be allocated. However, under Azadism there are some restrictions to this relating to the NAP in order to avoid some undesirable markets arising that destroy human freedom[10].

As we can see prices are the essence of the market, and any state manipulation of these through artificial price controls can lead to surpluses and shortages. A government backed price control system contributes most to the inefficiency in allocation due to the principles of supply and demand being distorted. If the state says no one can sell over a certain price then shortages occur since there is less incentive to produce that product. If it mandates that no selling is allowed below a certain price then surpluses (and waste) arise since there is a guaranteed above natural price payout for that good and so more people want to sell it[11]. Azadism does away with needless and ineffective government interference with natural market forces. Free market interactions, absent of state intervention, are a self-regulating system that requires no central authority determining where resources should go. It is the people themselves determining resource allocation through the voluntary interactions with each other. When something becomes scarcer, it becomes more expensive and because of this price signalling, people will demand it less. This will remain the case till suppliers are able to produce more and bring the prices back down through competition. Not only does this mitigate the hazards of bad economic policy, but also allows a better probability that resources will be used efficiently in respect to what people in a society actually need or want, rather than what a central planning authority decides for you. Why do you need someone you have never met, who has not lived any of your experiences, to decide what's best for you? And even if they are representative of you and your community, it is very unlikely that they will represent everyone else due to the sheer diversity of thoughts, needs and wants in a society. This does not justify the so-called "representative" to take off a certain group in order to meet the needs of another. In any other situation, that so-called "authority" would be labelled a thief.

Another way to combat scarcity is by reducing wants and needs of the people. However, achieving this is far harder than it may seem. Religions have been trying this for thousands of years. Even if desire for unnecessary goods and services were eradicated, people still need food, water and shelter. As the population grows, so does demand for these bare necessities. It is unreasonable to build a society on the assumption that when it is set up everyone will turn into Mahapurakhs and leave all worldly attachment and subsist only on air. The reality is that the vast majority of the world live in a state of Kalyug, and idealistic societies where everyone can just stop consuming only exists in Satyug. This is not to say that those ideals should not be strived for, but it is to say that to get there requires spiritual progress which must be done independent of state coercion. You cannot force anyone to be spiritual, so a society that builds upon the "lowest common denominator" of spiritual attainment is the only reasonable and realistic option in the meantime.

ਕਲਿ ਕਾਤੀ ਰਾਜੇ ਕਾਸਾਈ ਧਰਮੁ ਪੰਖ ਕਰਿ ਉਡਰਿਆ ॥

The Dark Age of Kali Yuga is the knife, and the kings are butchers; righteousness has sprouted wings and flown away.

— Sri Guru Granth Sahib, Ang 145

To conclude this section, a final example to showcase the broadness of markets is the concept of language. The revolutionary Austrian school economist and philosopher, Friedrich Hayek, elaborates that it is a mistake to think that language was thought up by wise men of the past[12]. Instead language development is a result of millions of interactions between people, each adjusting and adopting vocabulary as needed. If enough people call something by the same name, it was known by that label and added into an unwritten societal lexicon, common to all. If certain mouth noises were unpopular, they never became formal words. There was no authority decreeing what constitutes as language or mere noises. Instead, it was the independent, voluntary market transactions between the people themselves, who traded words to reach a mutual benefit in what was considered language. Only afterwards, were dictionaries written, not to invent language or even set the boundaries of language, but to record what was already in existence. The history of the first Oxford English dictionary was a monumental effort to scour through every major document and piece of literature available to them at the time. Although the first editions were finalised in 1928, the nature of having a dictionary for a "living" language means that it will never truly be finished until the language itself falls out of use. This is why even today words are still being added as society continues to engage in the trade of words and phrases[13].

Azadism promotes individual responsibility on the people themselves, and in the process removes the over reliance on the state to manage people's lives. People should be free to interact with each other in order to reach a common consensus without the need of a central planner dictating what is best for them. The only role of an Azadist government is to maintain the freedom of those interactions and protect the market's existence from any external or internal threats. Any interaction of a coercive nature would be dealt with as a threat to the functioning of an independent and free market. In any market interaction where one party is not satisfied, the other party cannot force the transaction to go through without breaking the NAP. This also applies to any market interactions between two parties that effect a non-consenting third party. Wherever the NAP is broken, it is the Azadist government's role to protect those affected and punish the aggressors. The primary function of the government is therefore largely limited to the justice system, police force and military. This inadvertently means that an Azadist government is a small one, and most other services are provided by the market and not the state.

Public sector

noun

1. the part of an economy that is controlled by the state.

Private sector

noun

1. the part of the national economy that is not under direct state control.

Oxford Dictionary

Private Vs Public

People Vs the State control of trade and resources

At the end of the previous section, it was stated that an Azadist government was a "small" one. This is not referring to the number of officials (although it can include this), but to the level of influence a government has in an economy. This naturally means that Azadism is placing more responsibility on the people themselves to provide most of society's services. In other words, public services are replaced by the private sector.

Initially many who are reading this may have a negative reaction to a larger private sector and may look to examples of the UK's NHS and compare it to the "private" healthcare system of the USA in order to highlight the failure of privatising industries. Another criticism may be that monopolies may enter and take over the market, thereby exploiting the consumer. This section will explain the fallacy in this way of thinking and will present a view that the private sector can not only outperform the public sector, but also do it in a way that maintains individual freedom and provide the best outcome for both consumers and producers.

Langar, Dasvandh and Choice

To help break the negative connotations associated with private industry, this section will begin by explaining why the institution of "Langar" is indeed a *private enterprise[1]* and not a public one. Langar is an effort where *private* individuals in a community come together and contribute *voluntarily* to provide free meals to whoever wants it. This forms the basis for the spiritual purpose of Langar as being a communal kitchen designed to not only just feed the community, but also provide an avenue to express and develop spirituality in a real way in terms of *Seva*.

Using the Oxford dictionary definitions of private sector and public sector, it is easy to see that Langar is designed as a private effort and operates absent of any state intervention[2]. There is no need for government involvement. There are no taxes that must be paid, there is no state mandated diet or regulation enforced on the process. Langar is managed solely by the private sector, or in other words, the community themselves organise this through voluntary action. People choosing to participate in this are free to donate as much or as little as they want or help in a variety of other ways absent of any state pressure or threat of punishment. The only authority in this is the *private* religious institution itself which may own the building and sets the dietary requirement or run the day-to-day management of the Langar. The reason why this authority is different from the government is because it is completely voluntary to participate in. Being private means that it has no legal authority over people who have decided through their own choice not to participate in it. The Gurudwara cannot forcibly collect donations or allocate labour, instead it relies on the community to take this up through their own individual choice. If the Gurudwara management recognises the need for more funds or help it can only ask its community. Unlike the state, the Gurudwara does not rely on the threat of force in order to coerce people into participating.

Whereas having a government managing this means that everyone *must* participate regardless of individual choice. This is because this effort would have to be funded through taxes instead. The core essence of Seva is eroded when people are forced to contribute, rather than contributing out of their own compassion. Deciding to sacrifice their own time, money and/or effort should be a decision made independent of state influence. Otherwise, in principle we are suggesting that the state must enforce its ethics on others. The first section already briefly mentions the dangers of giving the state a monopoly on setting ethics beyond a non-aggression principle, and this will also be expanded in a later section. In addition to this, we must ask ourselves whether forced ethics is truly what Sikhi promotes? Does the state forcing participation in Seva increase the spiritual benefit of it? Would paying for Langar through taxes hold the same personal spiritual satisfaction as paying for Langar through a voluntary donation? Gurbani actually already clearly provides us this answer, however this will be saved for the later section delving deeper into the nature of taxes.

It may be argued that the Gurus themselves had "taxed" the Sikh's through the concept of Dasvandh, but this is a critical mistake. One of the most important points that we must distinguish is the difference between taxes and Dasvandh. Dasvandh is a voluntary donation whereas tax is a non-voluntary payment that is collected either through force or the threat of force. There are no examples in Sikh history of the Guru forcibly collecting Dasvandh off Sikhs[3]. It may be said that Dasvandh is an obligation for every Sikh, the same way how tax is an obligation for every citizen. However, there is no obligation to be a Sikh. The Guru has never forcibly converted anyone into Sikhi, they instead relied on the veracity of their argument and lived what they preached in order to inspire and persuade the population to live a certain way. This is supported through the story of 40 Mukte where Guru Gobind Singh permitted the apostasy of 40 of his Sikhs (who later repented, returned, and achieved martyrdom). Additionally, Bhai Gurdas Ji in his Kabit Svaiye communicates the effort made by the Guru in order to reach his Sikh. However, the initial step in that direction is always down to the Sikh, thereby highlighting the voluntary, non-coercive nature of adopting the path of Sikhi.

ਚਰਨ ਸਰਨਿ ਗੁਰ ਏਕ ਪੈਡਾ ਜਾਇ ਚਲ ਸਤਿਗੁਰ ਕੋਟਿ ਪੈਡਾ ਆਗੇ ਹੋਇ ਲੇਤ ਹੈ ।

A disciple who walks one step towards Guru to take his refuge and goes to him with devotion and humility, Guru advances to receive him (devotee) by taking million steps.

ਏਕ ਬਾਰ ਸਤਿਗੁਰ ਮੰਤੂ ਸਿਮਰਨ ਮਾਤੂ ਸਿਮਰਨ ਤਾਹਿ ਬਾਰੰਬਾਰ ਗੁਰ ਹੇਤ ਹੈ ।

He who unites with the Lord by remembering the incantation of the Guru even once, the True Guru remembers him millions of time.

— Bhai Gurdas Ji, Kabitt Svaiye, Kabitt 111

An individual has the complete freedom to join the Sikh faith and part of the expected traditions may include paying Dasvandh. Since the initial decision to be Sikh was voluntary, any other obligations that stem from this, such as keeping Kes, taking Khanda Di Pahaul and Dasvandh, are also thereby a voluntary decision at its core[4].

Competition

In brief, Charles Darwin's theory of natural selection outlined that organisms on earth have been constantly competing to survive for billions of years. The constant struggle to survive and reproduce has propelled life on this planet from simple microbes to the complexity of human beings. None of this would have happened without *competition*. Organisms compete for food to survive and compete for mates to pass on their genes. Only those organisms that were able to adapt to their environment adequately and out-compete members of other species as well as their own, were best able to survive. Due to their adaptations, these organisms were able to obtain nutrition as well as reproduce to pass on those features that allowed them to out-compete. Those that were not able to do so died out. This meant that only those organisms with the right adaptations passed down their advantageous genes. The best characteristics from the previous generations were passed on and unhelpful features were eventually filtered out. This process of natural selection fuelled the evolution of the microbe with its simple biology, to eventually give us human beings with sophisticated systems and features such as eyes, brains, and even higher levels of consciousness. All this evolution was achieved through *competition*.

By seeing the economy similarly as an ecosystem, parallels can be drawn between natural selection and competitive free markets. The businesses are the organisms, and the competition between them is the natural selection. Only those businesses that are able to provide goods and services at a price and quality that there is a consumer demand for are able to survive and out-compete. Businesses compete by inventing new technologies, adapting and improving existing ones, or by finding more efficient methods of production. This constant striving to get ahead of competitors drives innovation and leaves consumers with products and services of a better quality and at a better price. In this sense, innovation is evolution.

For organisms, their success could be measured by the food or mates they obtained; the private sector hinges on the ability to generate profit. This inevitably leads to a private sector that is based on a profit maximising motive for the most part. Considering common conceptions of the term, this may initially seem unethical. However, looking at what profit actually is measuring, it is simply how well a particular enterprise or effort is able to minimise costs and raise income. If something is costing too much and simultaneously returning too little, this is an inefficient use of resources. The same way, if an animal spent more energy in obtaining food than it received from the consumption of it, then it will not last very long with this energy deficit. A loss is the market's way of communicating that this use of resources is inefficient and that the organiser of this venture should probably stop[5]. Similarly, the profit is also signal showing which use of resources is meeting the market's demands. As well as this, two businesses of similar nature can be assessed for their efficiency to manage the same resources by looking at how much profit each makes. The one with the most profit generally indicates a higher degree of efficiency. This does not then mean that a company can act in socially unacceptable ways to achieve maximum profits, such as cutting costs that dramatically reduces working conditions. In a highly competitive industry where there are low barriers to entry, the labour force has more of a choice in where to work and so a company offering too low wages, poor working conditions, minimal benefits (as compared to the rest of the market) will naturally cause people to have less incentive to work there. The company must reach a balance between cost reduction and maintaining competitive, all the while raising a profit. If it is unable to do so, it will be outcompeted by those that can. Again, over time, this harbours an environment of constant improvement since those that cannot meet this standard are filtered out.

Another example we could highlight is that companies may use unethical methods to acquire resources in the first place. Under Azadism, there are two possible solutions to this scenario. Firstly, if the means of accessing resources breaks the aforementioned "non-aggression principle", then it is the government's duty to stop this and prosecute the offenders. This shouldn't be some petty fine that they could easily pay and consider as just another business expense. It should be strict enough that provides a negative incentive towards breaking the law in this way. Secondly, these methods of production must factor into the decision making of the consumers themselves. The product is the result of the process of manufacture. If a clothing brand uses unethical means in its production process and consumers continue to buy the products despite knowledge of this, then they also must take the blame. The company also cannot legally hide this information either and so when it is inevitably exposed it will be punished through the justice system. Establishing when and where the NAP is broken is the sole role of the courts of an Azadist state.

On the other hand, public sector institutions break this framework entirely. When industries are "nationalised" and become part of the public sector, the state takes ownership over where the resources should go. This is putting power of resource management into the hands of a small group which would have otherwise been in the domain of the private sector, or in other words, the people themselves. Nationalised industries can then offer the illusion of a "free" service since the income of a public enterprise is coming from taxpayer's money instead. Since tax is obtained through force and not choice, there is no true way to gauge demand for public goods and services and adapt supply, because a public organisation receives an income regardless. The laws of supply and demand that gave way to price signalling is no longer present in a public company, and so it is far more difficult to use resources efficiently and allocate them to where they would be used best. The costs are also passed off to the taxpayers, which leaves very little incentive for a public company to be efficient or innovate. In a private competition model, if an organisation was misallocating resources, another private company could offer an alternative and capture demand instead. The same is true for the quality of a service or product. For a private enterprise it must constantly strive towards providing the best possible to avoid being out-competed, however a state-backed enterprise has no similar incentive. Under competition, if a business was better able to reduce costs to provide the same or a better quality product, they can reflect that saving in the price they charge. Thereby outcompeting the more inefficient business whilst providing the same or a better option to the consumer. The incentive to make a profit and to remain competitive by providing the best product available remains best realised in the private sector. Public sector organisations do not have this same drive since they have no competition. If they do, it is very difficult for a private firm to compete with something that provides a "free" service due to the state's "business costs" being paid for by the taxpayer and its income generated through the forcible acquisition of funds. If anything, it is *unfair* competition in this case, propped up and supported by the state using money they forcibly collect off the same consumers they sell to through taxes. It is essentially taking away the ability for the people to decide themselves where best to put their own money and putting faith in the government to best meet their needs. To re-emphasise, the ideal government's role under Azadism is to maintain a healthy, competitive, and fair free-market economy that functions within the boundaries of the law. As soon as it overextends its role as a safeguard for the market and instead becomes a participant, the rise of unfair advantages is an inevitability.

For the Sikh Panth, competition is nothing immoral nor even a foreign concept. As Sikhs we have been competing in every aspect since our inception. From Guru Nanak conversing in debate with the Yogis and Siddhas (which later on formed the basis of Jap Ji Sahib), Guru Angad Dev establishing the Mal Akhara at Khadur Sahib, encouraging the Sikhs to wrestle with each other and become familiar with combat[6]. Guru Hargobind Sahib "competed" with the Mughals in multiple battles, Guru Gobind Singh also followed this example, as well as promoted competition between his court poets through offering vast rewards of land and gold. Competition is nothing unethical in of itself, it is only the people competing who can engage in moral or immoral methods. Competition is merely the nature of things.

ਤੁਮ ਹੀ ਦਿਨ ਰਜਨੀ ਤੁਮ ਤੁਮ ਹੀ ਜੀਅਨ ਉਪਾਇ ॥

You [God] are the day, the night is you, you yourself created all living beings

ਕਉਤਕ ਹੇਰਨ ਕੇ ਨਮਿਤ ਤਿਨ ਸੈ ਬਾਦ ਬਢਾਇ ॥੯॥

To watch this drama, disputes were made [by God] to arise ||9||

...

ਪ੍ਰਿਥਮ ਉਪਾਵਹੁ ਜਗਤ ਤੁਮ ਤੁਮ ਹੀ ਪੰਥ ਬਨਾਇ ॥

First you created the world, you yourself established the paths

ਆਪ ਤੁਹੀ ਝਗਰਾ ਕਰੋ ਤੁਮ ਹੀ ਕਰੋ ਸਹਾਇ ॥੧੫॥

You yourself create conflict, then you yourself also help them ||15||

— Sri Guru Gobind Singh, Shastar Naam Mala

This may seem destructive and selfish initially, however when applied within the context of the law it can bring about great leaps in innovation and human flourishing. Often great achievements are produced in times of hardship. When a human being is in a competitive environment they strive to work harder and unlock levels of success previously thought to be unobtainable. It is for this reason that Sun Tzu in his 'Art of War' suggests the strategy of placing your forces in deadly situations, where they have nowhere to run (something that Robert Greene calls the *death-ground* strategy[7]). By putting your forces in a position where they cannot escape, they have no other option but to fight. This inevitably makes them fight harder than they otherwise would and creates a better odds of success.

> *"For it is precisely when a force has fallen into harm's way that is capable of striking a blow for victory."*
> —Sun Tzu's Art of War, ss. 11.59: The Nine Situations[8]

However, this does not just apply to life and death scenarios. Competition in general creates a sense of urgency, which is crucial for driving human beings to success and being productive in general. Consider the motivations of someone who has no sense of urgency compared to someone who does. How many students would complete their assignments with no hand in date? It is far more likely if you have a goal, someone to beat, deadlines to meet, an obstacle to overcome that you will use your human potential to its fullest[9]. Even the Guru employs this strategy in Bani when trying to get people to do their bhagti[10]:

ਰਸਨਾ ਰਾਮ ਰਾਮ ਬਖਾਨੁ ॥

With your tongue, chant the Name of the Lord.

ਗੁਨ ਗੋਪਾਲ ਉਚਾਰੁ ਦਿਨੁ ਰੈਨਿ ਭਏ ਕਲਮਲ ਹਾਨ ॥ ਰਹਾਉ ॥

Chanting the Glorious Praises of the Lord, day and night, your sins shall be eradicated. ||Pause||

ਤਿਆਗਿ ਚਲਨਾ ਸਗਲ ਸੰਪਤ ਕਾਲੁ ਸਿਰ ਪਰਿ ਜਾਨੁ ॥

You shall have to leave behind all your riches when you depart. Death is hanging over your head - know this well!

ਮਿਥਨ ਮੋਹ ਦੁਰੰਤ ਆਸਾ ਝੂਠੁ ਸਰਪਰ ਮਾਨੁ ॥੧॥

Transitory attachments and evil hopes are false. Surely you must believe this! ||1||

— Sri Guru Granth Sahib, Ang 1121

Additionally, competition isn't always a game of trying to defeat others. Instead, it is possible to foster an environment of good sportsmanship and mutual benefit from competition. Competition naturally results in highly effective forms of *cooperation*, they are not opposing ideals. Companies are organisations full of individuals constantly working together within a voluntary framework. The better those individuals can work together, the higher the chances of them all collectively outcompeting other collaborations. In fact, even by saying "outcompete" it wrongly implies that there must be one "winner". When choosing what phone to buy, you may have gone through many different options, comparing each with your budget, or the features you want. However, the one you finally decided on was your own personal winner. There does not need to be one universal winner for everyone since everyone has different preferences. Chairman of the Ayn Rand institute, Yaron Brook, commonly uses the example of Apple and Samsung[11]. Although these are both fierce competitors in the smartphone industry, the iPhone still uses many components manufactured by Samsung. Both parties benefit from this, and so do their employees who receive a regular income as well as the consumers who receive the products. The products would have been more expensive if this collaboration did not exist, since Apple would have had to build those components from scratch. The products are also constantly improving as a result of competition constantly innovating, and those innovations get used by everyone. Instead, both Samsung and Apple benefit from this trade, as well as the consumer.

Trade in general is a form of societal collaboration and cooperation. To illustrate this, an essay named "I, Pencil" written by the founder of the Foundation for Economic Education, Leonard Read explained the sheer complexity of producing a simple pencil[12]. This meditation of sorts explored the process and ultimately concluded that no one person on their own can produce even one modern pencil from scratch. The wood may seem reasonable to carve into the correct shape, but what about inserting the graphite? What about obtaining that graphite in the first place and getting it into the right size and shape? The metal that holds the rubber too is an insanely difficult process, where you would need to mine the ores and produce the right alloys. How would you do that without the foundries and heavy machinery? The rubber needs to come from somewhere too. In fact most of these raw materials come from all over, you would be extremely lucky to find them all in the same place, so factor in the cost of travelling as well. So many production processes would have to be mastered. Even if one person could know the entire process, it would still cost millions to extract, process and combine all these materials. This is just one pencil, imagine trying to produce another one that is identical.

However, through trade, we are able to produce billions of these pencils every year. Each part of the process is instead handled by different groups of people around the world. Countless people are involved in the process, each working on a specific area, specialising in their craft. This often involves hundreds working together to produce just one element of a pencil. However, no central planner determines any of it. Each person in this process only looks after his own self-interest. The lumberjacks cut the trees with no knowledge of where it will go and how it will be used. That wood is then processed by another group of people, equally clueless about the many uses of the wood after them. All these people are just trying to get paid for their work. Getting the tree to the wood processors is in itself a mystery. How were the trucks made, or the rope to secure the timber? Even basic things, like the clothes the workers wear or the food to feed them. These themselves have countless processes to get them too - a central planner would go insane! Yet, through this decentralised process, with everyone only needing to focus on their own tasks, innumerable pencils are produced and sold at a price that is only a fraction of the cost. Competition further streamlines all of this and encourages producers to be more efficient and satisfy not only the requirements for a pencil, but countless other things in order to generate a profit.

You cannot make everything yourself. Even the simplest things we take for granted are a result of worldwide collaboration between diverse groups of different religions, cultures and ethnicities. Through trade, people who would have otherwise killed each other now work together, whether knowingly or not. They have no combined purpose, nor need for a central planner to organise their efforts. If there is a demand for something, they will supply it in order to meet their own needs. Therefore, Azadism recognises competition as a form of cooperation as opposed to the coercive elements of when government interferes with the everyday transactions of the people. It is an alternative to just killing and stealing what you want, and instead encourages people of all walks of life, around the world to collaborate together whilst maximising human potential.

Regulations

To most, an unregulated free-market would be considered a nightmare of exploitation and corruption. Regulations may seem necessary to moderate the so-called "chaos" of the market and force people to behave in a desired way. In fact, a lot of blame is placed on the government for not regulating enough, so to have avoided "market" failures in housing, pollution, banking and elsewhere. Consequently, regulations may seem like an obvious solution to help protect the consumer. But let's pick one of these market failures to see how regulating them worked in the real world[13].

Housing has become increasingly unaffordable. Prices have risen at a rapid rate whilst home ownership is in decline, leaving many with fewer options. On the surface, this may seem like an obvious failure of the market and that government needs to step in and regulate this. However, lets first recall how prices are determined. If a supply of a good is limited, but the demand for it increases, this inevitably corresponds to increased prices. With the current housing markets, supply has not been able to grow fast enough to meet the greater increase in demand for them. But why is this? Government regulations actively hamper the freedom of building homes or restructuring existing ones to accommodate different living circumstances. Builders need to factor in costs of complying with regulations such as materials or the extra time and effort spent on meeting these standards. This inevitably gets passed down to the homeowner since these costs are incorporated into the final price they must pay for purchasing property or renovating. Alongside this, strict planning permission and zoning laws further increase the difficulty in making appropriate property types available. Through these restrictions the supply is actively suppressed to meet the market demand[14].

Under normal market conditions, a sudden rise in demand may in the short-term raise prices, but those responsible for building houses would now have more of an incentive to build more of them (i.e. new entrants enter the market). This is because the rise in prices translate into higher returns. As the supply rises to meet the demand, the price begins to fall and return to a natural level. As the price falls, the suppliers make less, thereby rebalancing the rate of construction. The problem is that regulations actively inhibit this process. As population is increasing, the demand for houses is going to inevitably rise, and so the supply needs to match this increase if society wants reasonable prices. A government regulating this process manually without the system of price-signalling already integrated in the market, leads to inefficiencies. Making too many homes will lead to low prices but many empty properties and a huge waste of materials that could have been used more productively elsewhere. Making not enough houses available is the situation we are in now, with decreasing affordability and fewer options.

At this point it may be reasonable to suggest price-controls, where the government sets the prices instead of the market forces of supply and demand. But this too is a critical error. Economists almost universally agree on this issue, that implementing a regulation on the prices of goods and services lead to shortages or surpluses[15]. By imposing a price floor too high, the quantity supplied increases even though the demand is not there. In this case usually government has to buy the product creating a guaranteed income for suppliers, who then continue to produce as much as possible and create wasteful surpluses. The government too can only buy these surpluses using tax-payers money, so ultimately the consumer has to pay for it anyway, just not directly. On the other hand, setting a price-ceiling too low, the supplier has less incentive from producing those goods since they can either not cover their costs or generate a substantial enough profit to justify the effort. Usually then the products that are supplied are of lower quality to reflect cost saving behaviour. Applying this to real life scenarios, cities and states around the world have experimented in implementing rent controls to control the rising prices in their rental markets. Inevitably, this led to far worse outcomes than before as affordability declined even further alongside a degrading of quality of the homes offered. In cases like New York city, this has been eased in over the decades so the harmful effects did not materialise immediately. However, both property prices and rent continued to rise to unprecedented levels. Those rental properties that were not subject to rent controls actually rose in price too, far higher than they otherwise would have without regulations. The reason being that rent controls actually ended up further exacerbating the issue of limited supply by taking more properties off the market and into the scheme. With the demand still increasing, the price in the market had to rise. Not only did this policy harm the affordability in general for everyone, but also harmed the very people it aimed to help. The tenants of these rent-controlled properties are effectively stuck as the market prices rise around them and price them out. Their only options are then to stay in their current property and continue to pay below-market rates or leave entirely. Since landlords cannot raise profits as easily through rent either, they cut corners and keep quality at a minimum to save on costs. This isn't just because they are greedy but often are unable to raise enough income to outweigh their outgoings. The tenant is then living in worse conditions than before, and they cannot force the landlord to do anything since the waiting lists for these homes are so large they can be easily replaced. In some places these lists have queued up to a level where people have to wait up to 20 years[16]!

So instead of this being seen as market failure, after drilling down into the details, this is actually one of many cases of government failure. First through stringent regulations in building homes the supply was artificially restricted. Then to fix this problem that they created, they tried to implement regulations on prices which further contributed to the shortages and led to lower quality housing for the poor as well as other social issues. Regulations caused the issue, and then they suggest more regulation will solve it.

But then how do we manage the harmful effects in the market? Many of these regulations must have come in the first place for a reason, how do we protect the consumer? Take the case of builders doing the bare minimum to the level that they cause structural instability and put people's lives at risk. Under Azadism a few measures are in place to help prevent this. The first measure is the NAP, upon which all law is based on. If the builders' work causes a collapse of a structure and lead to the damage of personal property or life, then they are liable for punishment. Under Azadism, this should be strict enough as to create a negative incentive for builders to erect such a weak structure in the first place. There is no need for state inspectors, since the builders themselves have an incentive to create safe structures so to avoid legal repercussions. The second measure is the builders' own market reputation. If a building company creates something that is of poor quality or ends up collapsing, then their reputation is tarnished. This directly effects their ability to generate future income since no one would want to hire them. The builders themselves have an incentive then to maintain quality and safe standards. This directly links to the third measure - *private* regulators. By privatising regulations, a market for trust develops. Instead of a government official acting as an inspector, the private sector establishes many independent inspectors competing to secure trust through exposing faulty practices. Now, the builders need to factor in a trust component as well when selling their services, and so would seek accreditation from these private regulators. By getting recognition of their standards from these independent bodies helps secure their reputations in the market as well as gives customers a sense of security[17]. The incentive to cheat and bribe inspectors may be compelling for some of these builders, however this is a risky strategy for all involved. Firstly, it would reflect badly on them if the inspector refuses the bribe, essentially dooming the company. Secondly, if the inspector is caught taking the bribe then the inspectors own reputation is destroyed and the market adjusts to avoid them both. Thirdly, the presence of many inspectors, all independent from one another increases the risk of being exposed, since all it takes is one inspector to call out a breach in standards. Compare this with government where if a private regulator is caught taking bribes, it will lose trust, fail and face legal charges. But if a government is caught, all it has to do is fire the employee. Private regulators therefore have a greater incentive to build and maintain trust and may find many innovative ways of proving themselves as they compete to increase reliability and truthfulness in their assessments. This may mean *private* certifications, licences[18] and other methods, all without the need of state interference.

Much of this already exists in terms of independent bodies and trade associations[19]. However, attention must also be given to simpler systems of regulation in the form of reviews. With the growth of the internet and social media, the medium in which reviews of products and services can be communicated has never been easier to access. Consider restaurants for example, a barrage of negative reviews can cripple the business. Great effort is put into maintaining a high standard in order to preserve and improve their reputation. Those restaurants with low quality food, poor hygiene and rude staff do not tend to last very long. Also consider, many of these review factors are also subjective. Some will cater towards different audiences and diets, and so reviews help communicate this too. Customer reviews have already formed a large part of the consumer's decision making process when purchasing goods, it is taken for granted how easily and widespread this practice is. From phones to clothing, almost every commonly sold item has a set of people leaving their opinions about them either on mediums like YouTube and Reddit, or even directly on the product's webpage itself. The role of reviews in a privately regulated system should not be understated nor restricted[20].

There are indeed market failures, but in the grand scheme of things, these are often rare, short lived and concentrated in small areas. Most of the time, by doing nothing the market resolves these itself. What tends to prevent this is politicians capitalising on the opportunity by convincing the people it is a failing of the private sector and that they must step in to help, even though it tends to be their fault in the first place. By even abusing the term "private-sector" they have successfully demonised it and implanted images of greedy business men. Private refers to the people directly, absent of state involvement. Farmers, entrepreneurs, charity workers, even our own Gurus are all private entities, acting separate from state influence. In fact, the Gurus fought hard to maintain this distinction and resisted state control in order to keep the public sector out of people's lives[21]. What the politicians are doing by blaming the private sector is saying to the people that it is their own fault for these things and only we can fix it. The reason why this works so well is that regulations are often "sound-good" policies designed to win over voters. Economist and Nobel Laureate Milton Friedman puts this best when urging attendees of one of his lectures to consider the consequences of regulations: "... we have to look at the actual consequences of policies not at the names of them"[22]. People often look at policy names rather than what they actually do, and this is what grants government greater and greater power. Also, note the similarity here with the Cobra Effect story from the first section. Often policy enacted in good faith leads to undesirable and unforeseen consequences when incentives are not considered.

"One of the great mistakes is to judge policies and programs by their intentions rather than their results."

— Mayagyani Sri Baba Milton Friedman Chicagowale

Whether this is done intentionally through nefarious actors, or simply as a result of incompetence, the outcome is the same. The people suffer and those who cause it offer more suffering to solve it. To stay protected against either, ignorance must be dispelled and replaced with knowledge. The more influence the state gains, the more it chips away at individual freedom until it is so inflated as an institution that "private" actors can infiltrate and use government as a tool to secure their own interests.

"Private" Monopolies

In economics, a monopoly is characterised as an organisation that has exclusive control over the supply of a particular good or service. Although, in reality there are very few examples of pure monopolies, this term usually refers to those corporations with large market shares. The primary concern with such entities is that they have overwhelming power in determining prices for their products and so nothing stops them to maximise their profits at the expense of the consumer. As a result, the people are worse off as they must potentially pay way above the natural market price.

By its nature, monopolies have few or no competition. Therefore, the remedy to a few firms controlling the market is to make it easier for new firms to enter it and compete. It may sound simple and obvious, but it is important to highlight that the real problem here is a lack of *competition*. If consumers were given more choice, then any one firm cannot simply hike up prices, since the consumer has the ability to go elsewhere. Or alternatively, they would also be free to set up their own enterprises. This provides an incentive for competing firms to provide the best price possible to consumers, regardless of their market share. In a free market, the only way they can maximise profit is by either increasing efficiency (lowering costs), offering a better-quality product, and/or convincing consumers to buy from them rather than someone else. Consumers are best protected from price manipulation and poor quality products in a competitive market in which there are many alternatives to choose from.

Hence, in order to combat and prevent monopolies, we must ask what exactly is preventing competition in the market? What is restricting the amount of choices available? A lot of this is down to the high barriers of entry into industries imposed through government intervention. These can be through such measures as discussed in the preceding subsection, namely: regulations, licenses, patents and tariffs. Initially, this may seem counter-intuitive, that regulations are exactly what we may need to curb the power of big corporations. But this is a mistake. Regulations are often the reason why such large corporations are able to exist at all. When introducing legislation backed by a threat of force (government), this creates a more difficult environment to compete in. The ability to pass through policies that grant an advantage now becomes a valuable resource, and so corporations seek to leverage this for their own benefit. Therefore, it is often the case that these barriers are set up by corporations themselves who influence government through a practice known as corporate political activity, and lobbying in particular[23]. This is where corporations are able to give money to the government in order to implement policies or grant exemptions that benefit them and give them an unfair advantage over the competition. Smaller businesses and entrepreneurs are unable to do this as effectively or at all, and so are more uncompetitive as a result. Rather than relying on the quality of their products or services, by adding a lobbying component into the mix, large companies are able to secure their market shares by actively hampering everyone else's ability to compete with them[24].

However, all the blame cannot just be placed on the companies. Politicians themselves use threats of legislative action to force companies to pay up too. Microsoft had resisted the use of lobbying for the longest time, until it was ultimately commercially infeasible to do so. The use of antitrust laws[25] by government were threatening Microsoft after they accused it of being a monopoly. These laws had the potential to impose crippling fines or even break up the company entirely. Acting similar to a protection racket run by Mafias, the government was giving them the choice to either pay-up or die. This inevitably led to Microsoft also engaging in these lobbying practices as a necessity and then the line of fire was directed elsewhere to other companies[26]. Now Microsoft has fully embraced corporate political activity and hire specialists devoted to lobbying[27]. Do not be confused about who is using who here. The lines between private and public sectors are blurred at this level as both the corporations and politicians benefit at the expense of the people.

By permitting lobbying, instead of solely competing for the consumer's demand, they compete for government favour. Small businesses cannot compete in this way, leaving a situation where large firms are left engaged in a bidding war to buy politicians or pass policies granting them advantages. If they don't their competitors will, or the government cripples them. The reality is that modern democracy can be bought and sold to the highest bidder when a government allows for lobbying. It is nothing other than an erosion on personal freedom and choice. Under Azadism, lobbying would be considered on the same level as bribery and so punished as a crime. Professions such as "corporate lobbyist" would be seen equal to the profession of a thief. Corporate interests should not translate into law, since this a disintegration of the distinction between the private and public sectors. When corporations are given the ability to set policy, they have essentially lost their "private" status. They are using tax-payer money to further their own interests and use the government to enforce their will on others, either directly or indirectly. This gives them an unfair advantage in the market over competitors and so lobbying is an active hindrance to the competitive free markets that Azadism is based upon. These practices in whatever form should be made clearly illegal as per the constitutional law of an Azadist nation. Whether its corporations influencing government, or the other way around, the very fact that one interacts with the other in this way should be avoided at all costs. Punishments should be severe for any violation in this area as it threatens the freedom of markets and ultimately harms the consumer.

Due to the restricted involvement of government in the market under Azadism, a government would not have the ability to enact many of these policies that the monopolies want in the first place. There are no government contracts, no special licenses nor regulations available for these corporations to manipulate. Large firms are forced to compete in the same free market environment as all other firms. If they cannot provide a service at a good enough price or quality, then they cannot continue to exist (as determined by the people, not the state). The sole reason why many of the largest corporations of our time are able to do so is purely due to their links with the state[28]. The only way to gain a large market share in this environment would be to offer a better product and a better price than all the rest. Given that value is subjective to each individual and dependent on everyone's own unique circumstances, so that preferences are almost always different, it is very difficult for a single entity to become a sole provider of a good or service. There are many factors that go into determining the subjective value of something for each individual which may go beyond the price of the product. This may include how the product was made, customer service, the goals of the enterprise, who is the provider or even the current mood of the consumer. This highly competitive environment, where anyone can set up a business, makes it far harder for monopolies to sustain themselves or become that large in the first place. The constant stream of competition is what best protects the consumer, not regulations that can easily be bypassed through lobbying. Especially not those regulations set up by corporations themselves. Any regulations that do exist should be private and not public.

However, it must be stated that there are indeed a few rare situations in which a "natural" monopoly can form under these conditions. And in these cases, it would not necessarily be undesirable for these firms to operate as a monopoly. Examples of this include:

New inventions: A company that has created something new would naturally have a monopoly over that product. Apple when they first released their iPhones effectively had a monopoly. However, seeing the massive success of this (and motivated by profit seeking), other companies such as Samsung also developed their own versions shortly after. Since then, the fierce competition in this industry has caused a boom in the rate of innovation of these products, the number of competitors (and therefore options), as well as the price for them decreasing.

Successful enterprise: Although unlikely, a business may be able to provide the best quality product at the best possible price and maximise its profit far greater than all other competition using the exact same resources. In this case, it is not necessarily harmful for anyone in this situation since consumers are willing to pay voluntarily at that price. If they start hiking up prices, then new competition would simply come back in to give consumers alternative options again, given that the market is free to enter.

Lastly there is the argument of predatory pricing. This is the claim that when firms get large enough, they can undercut competitors on prices by taking a loss for a period of time. When the other firms are unable to compete and leave the market, this leaves the predator firm free to raise prices. However, economist Thomas Sowell argues that this a flawed argument since the predator needs to have raised extra profit after the other firms leave the market in order to recuperate the losses it would have incurred using this strategy. When it raises prices to do this, competitors would enter the market again and offer the lower natural market price once again. Furthermore, if competitors go bankrupt, this does not mean all the equipment, buildings or workers suddenly "pop out" of existence. Instead, these are usually sold or hired at a discounted rate, and so other entrepreneurs are ready to take on this opportunity to compete. Lastly, if these tactics fail and competitors survive, all it does is leave the predatory business in a huge loss. These factors make it a huge risk for the predator firm to enact this strategy in the first place. What is more likely to occur are "price-wars" where firms compete to undercut each other by reducing prices, meanwhile benefiting consumers, as goods or services become more and more affordable[29].

To conclude, there are very few (if at all) purely private monopolies. What there are, is varying degrees and methods of state involvement in large market share organisations. It must be made absolutely clear that privatisation is not politicians passing on contracts to their friends. True privatisation under Azadism is the successful detachment between the private and public sectors entirely, where the strive is to meet consumer demand. I.e, winning the people's favour, not the politician's. Many industries of modern economies suffer from this sort of collusion between state and so-called *private* actors. Those who advocate for "Nationalisation" or to make private enterprise into public ones, are effectively promoting the formation of state-backed monopolies directly. In the following two parts of this section, two major examples of state-backed monopolies will be discussed in more detail.

Healthcare

One of the most important examples to discuss of state-backed monopolies is nationalised healthcare. Initially, private healthcare may seem like a worse offer than what is already present with public healthcare services around the world such as the National Health Service (NHS). It may be argued why replace a "free" system with a paid one? As mentioned previously, there is no such thing as a "free" government service. These are still paid for using taxes levied off the population. Although there is a moral problem with forcing people to pay for the healthcare of others, the same way as there is an issue with forcing any other forms of charity, there is another economic issue with having the state manage healthcare. Nationalised healthcare *is* a monopoly by definition, but in this case it is the government as the owners, and not a private entity.

Since any monopoly is in principle opposite to competition, there is less incentive to innovate and provide the best possible quality service. Due to the guaranteed income in the form of tax revenues, a public health system is paid for regardless of the performance or quality of service. By removing competition from the industry, market forces are no longer able to drive down prices and provide a better quality product. Innovation and efficiency suffers due to the lack of alternatives otherwise provided by a competitive free market, where drawbacks in one service would have led to opportunities for entrepreneurs to improve on. Instead, this allows mismanagement of resources to fester, and any failures with the service are often blamed on a lack of funding. What use is more money when the money being used currently is not being employed effectively or efficiently already? Simply throwing more money at a problem doesn't necessarily fix it, and so further resources are wasted in this pursuit.

In a market environment where healthcare providers must compete to provide the best quality service at the lowest possible price, those organisations that underperform are replaced by those that do. Only in a competitive market for healthcare is the wastage of resources best avoided, which is the same principle applied to all other industries. Healthcare should be no different, especially considering the longer lifespans of people, the emergence of deadlier viruses and new diseases. The societal need for healthcare to be constantly innovating to stay ahead these issues is paramount. Additionally, it is in the people's best interest to have the ability to decide between multiple alternatives. For example, if one healthcare provider fails to provide a quality service, and is plagued by poor doctors, racist nurses and long wait times, it is unlikely to exist for very long as people would generally avoid risking their health with a low quality provider. In addition, no two people have the exact same issue, and so having a system in which specialist practices can emerge to focus on treating specific problems would be desirable. This competitive environment may radically transform how healthcare is delivered in general. Allowing everyone to enter this industry increases the choices patients have, as providers are free to solve healthcare problems in unique and constantly innovating ways. It would then be up to the market to determine what works and what doesn't.

Entrepreneurs in India have already begun revolutionising the industry of healthcare in order to reduce costs and increase accessibility for even the poorest in society. The organisation *Glocal Healthcare* have done this by leveraging new technology and critically re-evaluating how primary and secondary care functions should be managed. They have set up small units in rural areas that provide key services such as check-ups and a digital pharmacy, which would have otherwise been done by hospitals in the cities by doctors and other professionals. Instead, these units can provide the same primary healthcare function at a fraction of the cost as well as relieving the pressure on doctors so they can re-allocate time in better ways for their patients. Rural populations have easier and cheaper access, and the issue of long wait times is tackled through the use of online video consultations directly with specialists and doctors from far away. Contrast this with the NHS in the UK which suffers notoriously long waiting times, lack of beds and general inefficiency[30]. It is clear to see how removing competition here drastically reduces its quality and capacity to innovate[31].

The US system should not be seen as the ideal alternative either. The reality is that the US government actually spends more on their supposed "private" healthcare system than the UK does, putting into question its private status entirely[32]. The obscene costs involved with healthcare in the US can also be quite clearly attributed to government intervention again, albeit in a slightly less direct way. For example, one of the reasons why medicines are so expensive is due to the government granting monopoly power to pharmaceutical companies through patents. This is a legally binding contract in which no other firm is allowed to produce a patented medicine for a set period of time. This means that when one of the pharmaceutical companies release a new drug, they become the sole provider of it and so have very little reason to keep prices low[33]. Another major problem is the barriers to entry into the healthcare industry set by heavy regulations. This reduces competition by increasing the difficulty of new healthcare entrepreneurs to enter the market and offer alternatives[34].

Although, it is important that medicines are trusted and should go through the necessary safety tests, it is not so essential that the government should be in charge of this. In fact, it may even be undesirable in many cases considering the track record of government "protecting" its citizens[35]. What Azadism offers as an alternative market solution is the *private* regulators mentioned previously. These act as reviewers who independently test and set their own safety standards of the drugs released by firms. The private regulators have an incentive to be truthful since their reputation and income depends on their ability to provide an accurate assessment. The pharmaceutical companies also then have an incentive to get their drugs passed by as many of these private regulators as possible in order to gain people's trust.

Under Azadism it is likely we would see an insurance-based approach to healthcare. People themselves would have to take the responsibility to purchase health or life insurance. Not only is this smart financial planning (especially for younger people[36]) but it also maintains the freedom of choice, as well as allowing for competition to flourish in both the healthcare and insurance industries. This may manifest in specialist packages that cover a variety of insurance options, for example whole family packages, or even the workplace offering plans as an incentive to attract employment. Market forces being free to work in this sector will also naturally drive down prices and increase the quality of the services offered, given that the government does not stifle competition. Furthermore, for those who still cannot afford this on their current wages, there are alternatives which will be discussed in a later section regarding social security. There is also nothing wrong with a town or community collectively deciding to finance an all encompassing healthcare system either, given that all funds are raised as donations and not taxes. This way they can similarly maintain a "free" service that is actually free because donations are a choice, whereas taxes are not. As long as people have the ability to choose and are not coerced in any way, the voluntary nature of this particular solution is more than acceptable under an Azadist system. All those who do not want to participate are free not to, and it is up to that particular healthcare provider to determine whether they will still offer assistance to them or not. This is in contrast to the current system in the UK where you have to pay "national insurance" regardless, and if you refuse you are kidnapped and thrown into a cage. The government has no need to be involved in any of these voluntary transactions. All it needs to do is step out of the way.

Education

Education for adults is another sector that should be constantly improving and innovating and therefore competitive markets here are also encouraged. However, for children this industry may need to stray away slightly from the free-market principles which underpins Azadism. So far, individual choice has taken the utmost priority, allowing the people to decide for themselves how best to spend their own money and live their own lives. However, this sovereignty over action can only apply to adults over an agreed age limit. In general, children are not completely developed mentally enough in order to make their own decisions without support from their parents. A child cannot rationally consent in market interactions, simply because they do not have the mental capabilities in order to make logical enough decisions for themselves[37]. Under Azadism, this diminished capacity to think means that they cannot enjoy the same right for self-governing and to exist within a NAP framework until they are over a certain age. Otherwise, a parent would have no legal way of forcibly managing their own child, as parenthood would demand NAP being broken all the time. How else can a mother feed her newborn? Would she have to first get consent, or draw up a contract and get the baby to sign it? Until the child has developed to a certain agreed age, they cannot have the same access to freedom in the sense that adults do. However, in the meantime to compensate, these rights are swapped with the right to education[38]. By Azadist law, every child born in an Azadist nation must be provided with schooling in the following fields as a minimum:

1. Maths
2. Language
3. Sports

The first reason as to why these must be provided to every child is that a child had no choice in being born. Therefore, Azadism would consider that it is the parent's duty to the child to give it the best possible opportunity to get to a stage where they are able to make their own decisions. By providing these basic fields of education, a child will be best able then to get to that stage of competency required for a sovereign lifestyle. The second reason as to why every child needs to attend a school is for their safeguarding.

Azadism considers every child in part, the shared "property" of both the community as well as the parent until adulthood. This is because a child cannot realistically defend themselves from their own parents (whether through neglect or ill intent) and so in order to prevent harm to the child, attendance at a school must be necessary. It may seem odd as to why a human child is referred to as "property", however this is only being used in the sense that there is ownership over them on behalf of their parents. When we say that a particular child belongs to their parents, we are inherently saying they are also property of them however not in the sense that they can be traded as a commodity[39]. Ingraining this understanding then allows us to apply the NAP based protections in the sense that any child that is harmed, is as if the property of the entire community is being harmed. Therefore, legal action is justified for these circumstances. This property status only lasts till adulthood, or cases of neglect where the parent half of the shared ownership contract is transferred to another set of guardians. Once reaching adulthood, the standard rights for protection under the NAP is applied as normal.

A school not only acts as a centre for learning, but a safe haven in which teachers have a dual role in teaching as well as ensuring the well-being of every child. If there are suspected cases of abuse, then it is the school's legal responsibility to raise this with the appropriate state authority in order to investigate. Those schools that actively ignore signs of neglect will be liable for legal action against them for the reason stated above. In addition, there will be a market reputation that a school has the incentive to maintain. If it is found out that a school is not able to protect its students from harm, the market is likely to adjust to this and move their children elsewhere. From a purely economics perspective, it is uncompetitive for a school to ignore abuse.

None of this requires any sort of public schools however, the only factors preventing this sector from being defined as truly private is the necessary laws set by the state to safeguard children and the minimum subject requirement. Beyond this, parents have the freedom to negotiate or find schools that offer curriculums they believe is best for their own child. To further enhance competition and facilitate freedom of choice under current systems, economist Milton Friedman popularised the idea of a voucher system. Instead of the state funding public schools, they would use that money to offer discounts to parents directly which can be used on sending their child to a school of their own choice. Friedman argued that the public schools should have nothing to worry about if they are providing a good enough service, and if they are not, why should anyone advocate that they should continue to exist[40]? Again, competition will allow those schools who best satisfy the demand of the people to prosper, and eliminate substandard schools which has been so damaging to so many, especially minority communities in the US and UK such as the Black diaspora[41]. However, despite this, Friedman still recognised a voucher system as only a "step" towards a free market solution to education[42]. Similarly, Azadism is not a static philosophy and so it also agrees with this as part of the inherent tendency to trend towards decentralisation and an eventual elimination of all government intervention. Although, a voucher policy may be an initial option for a state that wishes to transition into an Azadist economy, eventually even this should be abandoned to mitigate risks related to government intervention and involuntary funding of a programme through taxes. However, this does not mean the poor have to miss out. As will be expanded upon in a later section, the implementation of a form of universal basic income for low earners can act as an alternative to vouchers as another step towards the ultimate goal.

Furthermore, having private schooling mitigates one of the major risks involved with state education - *propaganda*. Private education minimises the risk of state propaganda and indoctrination techniques used in authoritarian regimes around the world, such as North Korea[43]. An Azadist government should have no role in determining what it feels that people should or shouldn't know, and especially *how* they know it[44]. This also helps reduce the power of states performing cultural genocide on minorities, by removing its power to set certain language requirements. It is down to the private sector, the people themselves, to determine what they want themselves or their children to learn (in addition to the basic requirements above). Countless times anecdotes of people are heard wishing they taught us this or that at school. In a private system, curriculums are set by parents (or students) and teachers communicating with each other directly, or even indirectly through price signalling. Just like any other business adapts to meet consumer demand, schools should also adapt to meet its clients demands also. If they can't, then people have the freedom to choose another school, same way if one business can't provide a service another can. Taking the state out of these negotiations gives this freedom and vastly mitigates the risk of state propaganda. The state should have no role in restricting ideas or history, and all subjects should be available for study as provided by the private sector. Market forces of supply and demand will be the governing factor in what is taught. For example, if companies start to increase their demand for engineers compared to a relatively low supply, the wages for engineers will rise. Seeing this, people may have more incentive to pursue those careers and therefore this increases the demand for education in that sector. Schools then in turn, seeing a rise in demand for this also make more courses available in order to make higher returns. In time, the supply of engineers rises to meet the demand and fulfil the skill shortage. This is simply the forces of supply and demand in action.

Since the market is free to provide education in a variety of formats, they will naturally compete to create the best possible way of disseminating knowledge. This does not even have to be in the form of diplomas or degrees in the traditional sense, and instead could be different certifications all together. Companies themselves can establish tests that potential employees must pass and so specific courses could be designed to concentrate on these rather than less relevant topics. This already happens to an extent amongst large firms who test candidates as part of the application process. This moves society away from one which encourages simply acquiring pieces of paper saying you spent a few years in a university, to one that values the actual skills and knowledge you acquired. Giving the education sector a profit incentive means that it has to focus on results, otherwise why would anyone go to a school with poor performance and low rates of employment for its students[45]? If no students go there then it simply cannot continue to exist since it cannot cover its costs. The end goal of creating a well-educated, employable and highly skilled student will take precedence. A state funded school has no similar motivation, since they are paid for regardless of performance. In fact, those with worse than average performance may be applicable for *more* funding, which completely reverses the incentive. Rewarding bad outcomes, perpetuates bad outcomes. Another potential system that is free to arise (or re-emerge), if there was sufficient demand, is the 'Gurukul' system of ancient India. This was where students went to live with a Guru and become their disciple (Shishya) and was primarily aimed at teaching scriptural knowledge, but would have covered other lifestyle aspects such as arts and music depending on the Gurdev[46]. This may be a great way to bring up children who were neglected especially, and give them an opportunity to learn about a variety of aspects of life, and not just the academics.

A final point must be raised about universities. Although on the surface these may seem like private institutions, they are indirectly funded by the state. The government provides guaranteed loans to students who then enrol on degrees with the hope that they will pay them off with the higher salaries they will earn as a result of the education they get. However, due to this the university realises that it will receive a guaranteed income regardless of their performance. This is the exact same danger that threatens innovation, quality service and natural prices as with state backed monopolies. Universities now have decreased incentives to compete for lower prices and better service, since they know they will get paid anyway. This is the primary reason why university education is so expensive, and rising. It is essentially free money from the government, and therefore the taxpayer takes the hit. The students are the ones taking on the inflated debt for this as they make repayments over the next thirty years of their working lives if they earn over a certain amount in the UK. If they are unable to pay it all back (which most don't)[47], the cost is further thrown on the taxpayer. Alongside this, there has been a societal push to get people into universities in order to capitalise on this scam[48].

Taking market forces out of the equation have left many students who are starting their lives with tens of thousands in debt and degrees that may not be in demand in the job market. Governments producing these loans may have had good intentions for doing so, but the outcome is turning into a disaster. University students themselves will highlight the struggles in finding work after graduating, even with in demand degrees. Since almost anybody can get these degrees, there is nothing special about having them anymore, meaning that students need to gain even more qualifications on top to be able to compete for jobs[49]. Additionally, companies are asking for work experience especially which further shows that having a degree in many cases is simply not enough. Apprenticeships are designed for this very reason, as they provide on the job experience and instead of accumulating debt, you are paid a wage.

Originally, getting a degree was a personal investment of time and money that was not pushed on to everyone to achieve, the risk was on you. It was a personal sacrifice taken on by the individual and not paid for by society as a whole in the form of taxes. Similar to healthcare, universities should not be another forced charity for people, and should be accessed just like any other business. As a result universities should be exposed to a market, where their price is determined by the quality of their service. Just as before, through competition, the quality will rise and the price will drop to the natural level. Students would be in a much better position financially and could realistically work part-time to help pay off any debts they may incur. Alternatively, there may be many other options to the university system in general. Similarly to the previous section, if people still desire a free education system for members of their community, nothing is stopping them from pooling their money together to fund the education of their members. As long as it is done voluntarily, through donations and not taxes, it is perfectly acceptable under an Azadist system.

To summarise, an Azadist education system is a private one and is free from state intervention. The only exception is the law requirements which mandates all children have to attend a school to study the minimum required subjects. Giving the people the choice is paramount in creating an effective education system under Azadism, however it must also be balanced with the correct safeguarding for children which can only be guaranteed through a mandatory schooling law in the beginning. Despite this, education providers must compete like any other industry and in the process this will create better service and lower prices for all. One way to encourage this at the start of a transition into a Azadist state from an existing system, may be in the forms of offering school vouchers to parents, or a form of basic income. The central government should not set any curriculum beyond the basic requirements for children. Even with this, it can be devolved into the state level or lower aggregations in order to further de-risk and decentralise power over time.

IV

Taxes, Welfare and Safety Nets

Reconciling freedom with providing social security.

Inequality and Poverty

The problem of income and wealth inequality has been present throughout history in many societies. The only difference is that in the modern age, inequality has taken a slightly different guise. Whereas, before it tended to be the rulers and nobles hoarding all the wealth and power, these days there exists private individuals with net worths greater than GDPs of entire nations. Although this is indeed a problem, it may not be in the way that it is initially assumed to be.

FIG 1

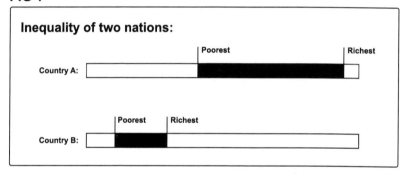

Figure 1 above shows the inequality between two nations. Although Country A has the larger inequality, the poorest are still richer than the richest of Country B. Despite its simplicity, the purpose of this example is to highlight a key component to this debate that is often overlooked. Inequality is a secondary issue to that of poverty. If everyone in a nation is getting richer, then in theory, it should matter less that some have made more money than others. The primary concern should be *how* they have made their money, not how *much*.

In the real world, there are many different measures for calculating economic inequality, one of the more popular being the Gini coefficient[1]. This measures the proportion of wealth held by a number of individuals in a nation. A Gini coefficient of 1 means that one person earned all the income (perfect inequality), where 0 would represent every person earning the exact same income. To highlight the concept of the above example using OECD data, the values for both Luxembourg and Spain are similar (0.327 and 0.333 respectively), yet when looking at GDP per capita, they differ greatly ($112,188 and $39,580)[2].

Inequality is not static either, just because someone is poorer now doesn't mean they will always be. Economic maneuverability is another important metric that must be considered here. In a research paper examining the likelihood of experiencing relative poverty in the US, Rank and Hirschl report on the periods of time in which people enter and remain in the bottom 10% and 20%. Their findings show that although 61.8% of people may enter the bottom 20%, after one year this rate drops to 38.2%. This then continues to fall, whereby only 5.6% remain in this percentile for 10 or more consecutive years[3]. For the bottom 10%, 42.1% enter this level for at least a year, which further reduces by roughly half to 20.5% after one year. Only about 1.5% stay at this level for 10 or more years consecutively. However, again this is relative poverty not absolute, which is an important distinction. Where absolute poverty is measured in terms of a set threshold level, relative looks at the bottom percentiles in relation to the average level of income of the population. This means that the poorest of a relatively high average income nation may have higher standards of living than the poorest of a lower average income nation[4].

The upper stratas also show similar levels of mobility too. 56% of Americans expect to reach the top 10% in their lifetimes, and 73% getting into the top 20%[5]. Of the top 1%, 11.1% of people are expected to reach this stage, however, this plummets to 4.5% after one year and only about 0.6% will remain here consecutively after 10 years[6]. There are a variety of factors that lead to these changes over the course of people's life: marriage, selling homes, losing or obtaining new jobs and much more. Despite this, it is common to hear the solutions of inequality follow more along the lines of forcible redistribution of wealth from the "1%" as if this was a fixed group of people "hoarding" all the wealth. However it is crucial to understand that this is not a *zero-sum game*.

One of the most prevalent economic myths is the 'fixed-pie' fallacy. This is the assumption that there is a fixed amount of wealth in this world, and so, if one person becomes wealthier it is because they have taken more from someone else. The same way a pie is fixed in size and must be sliced up and divided between recipients. If one person cuts a bigger slice for themselves, it naturally will leave everyone else with less. The problem is, however, wealth cannot be compared to a pie since wealth *grows*[7]. With every invention or innovation comes an increase in the amount or quality of goods and services available in society, often creating entire new industries in which people can enter and expand. Efficiency may also be increased as new ways of production are developed to better meet the demands of the people. As new areas of human potential are unlocked, previously unrealised opportunities become manifest. Jobs in less physically demanding areas become more accessible, and the fruits of this labour become increasingly rewarding. With better products and services available due to the societal increase in wealth, everyone benefits. It is often a mistake to judge wealth expansion solely in terms of money alone, since the range and quality of goods and services now available must also be considered. In wealthy nations, the poorest still have access to advanced technology such as smart phones, cars, fridges etc., all of which would have blown the minds of even the richest a hundred years ago. Increasing wealth for all as opposed to just a few is mutually beneficial for all parties involved. The fact that the market is structured in this way naturally creates an incentive to increase societal wealth as whole, since for companies especially this means more potential customers are available. As an entrepreneur, would you rather sell your product in an area of high wealth, or in a desert where nobody lives? By creating and sustaining positive feedback loops such as these the level of wealth increases.

FIG 2

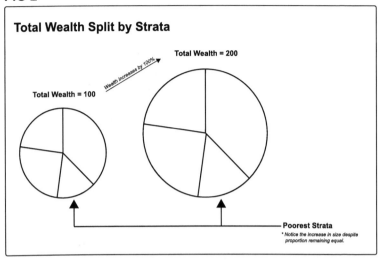

Statements such as "the rich are getting richer, and poor and getting poorer" are simply untrue. Hans Gosling through his work with Gapminder, revealed many misconceptions people have regarding the current state of affairs in the world[8]. He showed that many often think things are worse, or are getting much worse than they actually are. Some of the most striking examples of this has been regarding global poverty levels. Participants of their surveys were asked to pick what level of the world's population live in extreme poverty today considering that in 1980 it was 40%. 92% of respondents got this wrong, expecting a rise or less reduction than the actual level of 10%. Despite inequality increasing, the level of poverty has plummeted, alongside infant mortality rates, longer lifespans and general increase in quality of life[9]. A more reasonable conclusion based on the facts are that the rich are getting richer at a faster rate than the poor are getting richer - but we are all indeed getting richer[10]. Which makes sense. Those with more money, have more available to invest and grow. A 7% increase in £1 Million compared to £100,000, is far more in real money terms. Crucially, the rich are better able to capitalise from compounding interest especially, since they have more money compounding, or are even aware of the power of compounding[11] in the first place[12].

To see wealth as a zero-sum game is fundamentally flawed. Many have made this mistake, predicting that as the population increased, poverty would also as there would be less to go around[13]. The reality thankfully proved them wrong, as poverty has reduced drastically despite the boom in population growth over the last century. Human beings are not cattle or crops. We have the capacity to think and manipulate our environment in order to solve innumerable problems. Human ingenuity is the reason why you can read these words right now. Having more people means more opportunity to create wealth and innovate, thereby circumnavigating or at least reducing the magnitude of many great threats such as disease, natural disaster and war. Admittedly, innovation has brought its own problems as well such as climate change and superbugs, however this is just more reason to innovate further. To achieve this, a nation must nourish free thinking and give people greater opportunities to solve these problems by getting government out of their way.

Despite this, if the issue of overpopulation still seems concerning, solace can be taken in some of the other incredible work conducted by the Gapminder institute on this topic. Hans Gosling explains that the current predictions estimate that human population has begun to plateau and may peak at 11 Billion by 2100. In the past and amongst developing nations, the number of children per household averaged much higher than it is now. This was mainly due to the nature of work which required support from larger family units, and given the fact most children ended up dying before reaching adulthood, there was greater incentive to have more children in order to ensure that at least a few of them would survive. However, these justifications no longer hold as much weight as the world is developing. Thanks to advancements in medicine, hygiene and new work opportunities, more children are living longer and surviving. Increasingly, it is becoming more infeasible for the poorest to have so many children, since that is more mouths to feed. With education becoming more accessible, their children can attain better jobs away from hard labour, escape poverty and uplift their whole families. These reasons contribute to the diminished incentive to have so many children, and to give more focus to the ones people do have. Eventually the birth rate would likely reach an equilibrium with the death rate, and give the planet a constant population level of approximately 11 billion.

Although poverty has indeed dropped, it has not done so equally across all nations. When reading the above, your mind may have instinctively visualised families in some African nation or Bangladesh etc. This isn't racism. The fact is that the so-called "west" and other developed nations have seen unprecedented rates of wealth creation, and as a result their populations suffer far less from poverty. We can cry about this, complain and give all manner of excuses. Or we can learn from it and explore the real reasons as to why this disparity exists. If we really want to understand how to build a successful nation in which poverty is minute (if it exists at all) and the people are able to prosper and live free, we must understand the reality of the situation by putting aside emotion and adopting reason. It may be easy to stick all the blame for this on the colonial powers of the past few centuries, namely Britain in particular. However, something was unique about these invaders compared to the past. Many empires have risen and fallen, and many kings were able to amass great hordes of wealth through conquest and plunder. But these modern nations were able to keep hold of their riches in a far different way. By granting some level of *economic* freedom, wealth was more successfully disseminated amongst a greater proportion of the population outside the elites. This is not a defence of the British empire in the slightest, and in fact colonisation as a whole is strictly antithetical to Azadist principles[14]. The East India Company was a state-backed monopoly, granted exclusive trade rights in India by their monarch, which, as was discussed in the previous section, is completely opposite to what Azadism advocates. Alongside this, Azadists take a strong position that the British Empire (alongside many others) have ultimately caused vastly more harm than good. In fact any "good" that did come out of it was attached to costs so high it is ridiculous to suggest that any of it was "for the best". The sheer number of lives lost, families destroyed, cultures dismantled, religions distorted, and spirits crushed can have no compensation. The devastating effects, socially, economically, philosophically are inarguable for these invaded nations. Instead, what this analysis focuses on is what happened to that accumulated wealth in the invader's home countries. It is not so simple to say they just stole from other nations and this is why they became so rich, since in these cases it was not just the ruling classes that kept the wealth. It was used in a way that maintained that wealth and expanded upon it.

Many theories have been suggested as to why some nations are richer than others, as outlined in the opening chapters of Acemoglu and Robinson's book: 'Why Nations Fail: The Origins of Power, Prosperity and Poverty'. Race, culture and climate have all been used in the past to explain these differences, however geography in particular has been a particularly prevalent theory, and for good reason.

In Adam Smith's "The Wealth of Nations", chapter 3 goes through the limiting factors associated with the division of labour, in which he highlights the importance of transport in opening up trade and getting access to the world markets. He uses the example of ships revolutionising the transport of goods and services by allowing for more to be shipped, using less labour, over greater distances, and in less time than traditional horse and carriage. These factors allowed for the economies of the port cities to flourish far greater than remote in-land settlements, due to the greater access to other markets and a more efficient method of trade. Looking into the history of empires and nation-states, those that were situated on coastlines or had access to ports and the sea, tended to progress far greater than those that had not. Even today some of the world's most wealthy nations are city states such as Hong Kong, Singapore and Taiwan which have extensive ports and sea networks linked to them. Even Maharaja Ranjit Singh had ambitions to reach the ocean before the kingdom collapsed[15]. Alternatively, isolation has been repeatedly shown to prove disastrous in promoting prosperity. Thomas Sowell expressed the failure of isolationism as an economic policy by pointing out how historically, those societies that kept to themselves and avoided interactions with foreigners led to much diminished levels of success in comparison. Smith also eluded to this in his own time using examples of settlements and cities that were located further inland and comparing them to port towns, or cities located on shorelines or the banks of great rivers. These factors made trade far easier and thus wealth was better able to be transferred and grow, for the mutual benefit of all involved.

However, the geography hypothesis can only be taken so far, and although it may help understand the difference between cities and regions, it can fall short when scaling up to the level of nations. Acemoglu and Robinson instead reject this in favour of a new perspective, suggesting that it is the ease of access to *institutions* that is the most important factor. By pointing out a series of examples around the world of nations with similar geographies but with huge disparities in wealth, they put the idea that "some places are just better suited than others" under scrutiny. North and South Korea (despite their once vast similarities in race, culture and geography) could not be more different in their trajectories after their split. Why is this? The US and Mexico is another relevant example, with the town of Nogales being one of the case studies used in their book. This town is divided by a border, half in Mexico and the other half in the US. However, on the US side the residents earn three times more, have lower crime rates and live longer lives. The reason for this lies in the formation and subsequent development of these two nations. Mexico's land and resources was far superior to North America's, and its people were quickly enslaved. The Europeans landing further north though faced far more resistance, harder terrain and poorer land quality. Whereas the Spaniards to the south established institutions to exploit the native inhabitants and created a system in which to keep them merely on a subsistence level (and therefore reliant on their invaders). If not outright enslaved, they would be forced to work for low wages, pay high taxes and inflated prices for goods and services. This time-tested model expanded the wealth of the royal families and conquistadors, but at the expense of the economic prosperity of the nation as a whole.

The resource and labour rich southern regions being thoroughly exploited, the English arriving late were left with the inferior northern territories. Initially failing to replicate the Spaniard's policies, they instead were forced to grow their own food and trade. Their initial plan to kidnap the natives' king and hold him ransom was not viable, rather they had to negotiate and work with them (for now at least). Their intentions then turned towards exploiting their fellow colonists instead and so they set up a large corporation (the Virginia Company) who owned all the land and new settlers from Europe were then forced to work under grueling conditions in pre-defined roles and oversaw by company agents. Naturally people began to run away into the frontier and in response the company imposed death penalties for anyone caught deserting. Inevitably this system collapsed as people from Europe became aware of the situation, thus avoiding the lure. With the population dwindling, the Virginia Company had to change its tactics. Realising that the typical colonial strategy was not feasible for their circumstances, they instead granted land to their workers to cultivate on their own as well as rights to have their voices heard in determining laws via general assemblies. By giving the people (at least some of them) a stake in their own success, the system now geared towards an incentive based one rather than solely exploitation based.

Other colonies also began to spring up after being granted land by the English crown. The lords of these colonies were given freedom to experiment with different types of government structures, and after failing to implement the feudal systems that had existed in England, they too conformed to the principles on which the Virigina Company began to trend towards. The feudal system they failed to replicate was similar to the Mughal system in which lords were given ultimate authority over areas, and under them came tenants (or zamindars in India), which further delegated land and labour in order to raise taxes for the lords and state monarchs in return for wages[16]. Similarly to India, a pseudo-caste system developed with the lower classes being known as "leet men", and their children also inheriting their status. However, this again acted as a perverse incentive, and this system too collapsed in the US since there were more attractive alternatives in escaping to the frontier or staying in Europe. Eventually the colonies became proto-republics in a sense that each was governed by an assembly of all land owners within a district. These were far off the "democracies", or more accurately the republic, that came later on as they refused rights to Blacks, women and the poor[17]. However, it still was revolutionary for their time in terms of the broadness of political representation. Although rudimentary at this stage, it nonetheless marked the beginnings of a system in which individuals began to equalise wealth and power away from just the monarchs. This crucial restructuring enabled the North American colonisers to gradually pursue greater freedoms both economically and politically[18].

Mexico on the other hand drafted a constitution that preserved power amongst their elite classes. Although there was an effort to establish a proposal for popular representation in politics, it unfortunately failed to gather traction. Consequently, their society was structured towards catering for the top classes as a priority. Instead of empowering the common people, it geared towards consolidating monopolies and exploiting the native populace. It was only the wealthy who were able to access essential institutions and services such as acquiring loans, making it very difficult for ordinary people to start their own businesses and expand wealth. Combined with long lasting political instability, and therefore reduced capacity to protect private property rights, the economy of Mexico as a whole lagged behind. Alternatively, the US operated in a far more decentralised manner in terms of power, through senates and wider representation of the common man into politics. Albeit at a limited level, but still far greater than Mexico was at the time. This also enabled them to capitalise on the opportunities presented at the advent of the industrial revolution. One example of this is the broadening of who could acquire a patent as well as access to financial institutions[19]. Since patents were relatively inexpensive to acquire, it was easier for a poor person to have the opportunity to invent something new and bring it to market. The banking sector was monumental in facilitating this as it allowed access to finances. Since this sector was left largely unrestricted, competition flourished leading to banks being able to offer low interest rates on loans essentially making it cheaper to borrow money[20]. In the US there were 338 banks in 1818, growing rapidly to 27,864 by 1914. Mexico on the other hand had only 42 by 1910, two of which controlled 60% of the total banking assets. Due to the lack of competition, interest rates were much higher, effectively shutting off the path of entrepreneurship for Mexico's poorest. Therefore, only the already wealthy could feasibly access these services and they used it to consolidate their wealth and expand their influence to monopolise existing industries.

In the US, if someone had an idea, they were far more likely to get funding and freedom to try it, thereby enabling a greater proportion of the people to start their own enterprises. Naturally this then led to increased levels of competition amongst the private sector, leading to innovation and wealth expansion for all. Fundamentally, it is economic freedom that best maximises the chances for prosperity and the reduction of poverty. The *Index of Economic Freedom* developed by the Heritage Foundation, is a annual ranking that measures economic freedom in nations across the world. It takes into account the following 12 factors[21]:

Rule of Law	Government Size	Regulatory Efficiency	Open Markets
Property rights	Government spending	Business freedom	Trade Freedom
Government integrity	Tax burden	Labour freedom	Investment Freedom
Judicial effectiveness	Fiscal health	Monetary freedom	Financial Freedom

Many of these factors mirror what Azadism is concerned with, and by looking at how each indicator effects the overall score for economic freedom, we can get a good idea of how prosperity can be achieved. Refer to the Appendix to see exactly how an Azadist state aims to perform in each category.

When looking at nations around the world today, those that tend towards economic freedom show the least amount of poverty and the highest rates of prosperity. Some of the highest scoring nations on the index include: Singapore, Hong Kong, New Zealand, South Korea, Ireland and Switzerland. Although not perfect (as each has many issues of their own) these nations nonetheless currently best encapsulate Azadist principles and can be seen as real world implementations of many of the ideas presented in this manifesto. Combing low tax rates, reduced barriers to entry for businesses, strong enforcement of property rights, minimised corruption in government alongside other policies have led these nations to become some of the most prosperous regions in history - many of which started as insignificant fishing villages. Wherever freedom has been promoted, those societies improve, and freedom in the economic sense is a necessary part of freedom as a whole. The reason why these correlate is due to the increased wealth enabling far better access to resources and ways of working that give people many options in how to live their own lives. It is upon this, Azadism wishes to export prosperity to any region on the globe by providing similar formulas for success. However much a nation has trended towards freedom, it has equally seen a greater quality of life, healthier and longer lives as well as generally wealthier. By any metric we can measure, we have seen a rise in prosperity overall as the world has trended towards greater freedoms economically. It is imperative, therefore, that to eliminate poverty the trend towards freedom continues to rise. Even if inequality may rise as a by-product, the fact is that all are better off if wealth is grown under Azadist conditions as opposed to the system in which the colonial powers of the past employed.

This is not to say that inequality is not a problem, but instead, the major problem with inequality is its perception, and as a result social stability. It seems as though many people are accustomed to seeing the situation around them for what it is now, rather than the progress that has led to this point. It is reasonable to feel compassion for those going through difficult times and resentment for those that are in the complete opposite position. The fact that these are mostly temporary positions (on both sides) and have been getting better over time is often ignored. What this creates is a sort of social tension between the rich and the poor, which is not to be taken lightly according to Jordan Peterson[22]. This inevitably leads to a situation in which tribalism manifests, and groups compete to gain the government's favour to debilitate the other. In the process, the entire nation suffers. In fact, Karl Marx based much of his ideas off of this dichotomy, promoting the idea of a class struggle between the bourgeoisie and proletariat[23]. These notions went on to materialise as the horrors of the USSR in which groups such as the Kulaks were sent to Gulags and killed en-masse. Hitler then took these ideas further by applying his own racial tint by demonizing the Jews, using wealth as a key component of his arguments against them. So what is the best way to tackle it? Azadism suggests that a nation must increase mobility for the poorest in society to reach higher levels of income by removing barriers and maximising opportunity. The previous section delved into the specifics of the harms associated with artificial barriers to entry and restricting competition, whereas this section will now focus on how to best safeguard and promote those who are currently in poor financial positions. The more important focus is to alleviate poverty through maximising human potential, rather than to punish success[24].

"There's no doubt that inequality destabilizes societies. I think the social science evidence on that front is crystal clear."

— *Jordan Peterson*

To conclude this opening section to part 4 of this manifesto, contemplate this example from Ithiaas. On visiting their Gursikh, Bhai Lalo, Guru Nanak and Bhai Mardana were offered food prepared by the poor carpenter. The government appointed custodian of the village, Malik Bhago was made aware Maharaj's arrival and invited him to abandon the peasants hospitality and to partake in his feast instead. After initially declining, he brought with him a roti from Bhai Lalo's house. In one hand he held Bhai Lalo's and in the other Bhago's. When squeezed the former secreted milk, and the later oozed with blood. A powerful metaphor, highlighting the corruption of Bhago and the cruelty in which he treated his workers. Whereas milk symbolised the purity of Bhai Lalo's nature and hard work. The Guru saw Bhago's exploitation clearly and recognised his hubris and greed. The problem here was not his wealth, it was the means in which he obtained it. The later manifestations of the Guru controlled vast amounts of wealth relative to the average population of the time. Were they also immoral for being so rich? Wealth is only a tool, same way weapons or wagons are. The nature of those who use them should be the primary concern. Azadists should be concerned less with how much someone has, only how they obtained it[25]. If it was through breaching the NAP then it is illegitimate and only then it is deemed immoral. If it is through providing a good or service that people have willingly paid for, then no issue should be raised at a state level. It is not automatically true that someone who owns a lot of wealth is by default consumed by greed and attachment. When Raja Janak was told that his kingdom was engulfed in flames along with all his worldly possessions, he remained unmoved, preferring to listen to the sermons of his guru. Instead, it was the Brahmins who owned nothing but their Janeau and two sets of clothes (one set of which was currently in the burning palace), who ran to save their belongings.

ਭਗਤੁ ਵਡਾ ਰਾਜਾ ਜਨਕੁ ਹੈ ਗੁਰਮੁਖਿ ਮਾਇਆ ਵਿਚਿ ਉਦਾਸੀ।

King Janak was a great saint who amidst maya remained indifferent to it.

— Bhai Gurdas Ji Vaaran, Vaar 10

Taxes

The two primary functions of tax are:

1. Pay for public goods
2. Redistribute Wealth

The first function is largely defunct in an Azadist economy, since most industries are eventually privatised and handed over to the market. Most tax revenue would initially be used to uphold the government's main security and justice functions. However, even this should be eventually phased out over time to be replaced by a Dasvandh based approach. This subsection will largely focus on the second function on taxes.

Traditionally, to combat inequality in a society, it is common to hear that higher taxes should be imposed on the rich in order to give more to the poor. However the real-world implications of these sorts of "robin-hood" tactics have significant drawbacks[26]. Firstly, imagine raising corporate tax on the largest, most successful firms to force them to "give back". By excessively taxing these firms it becomes increasingly unprofitable for them to continue in that region and so they become more inclined to move their operations elsewhere. This negatively impacts the economy as they take with them the many benefits they provided in terms of employment, further investment and potential access to goods and services. So instead of having the intended outcome of increasing government tax revenue from that particular company, the state now takes nothing.

For example, if country A had a corporate tax rate of 50%, but B had a rate of 10% then logically, a corporation would want to operate in country B, since the cost to them to do business is far lower. Obviously, just like a real market, there would be many other variables that factor into these decisions such as political stability, geography, access to labour, etc. But taxes would indeed form a major part of this decision, as we have seen with many large firms moving headquarters to Ireland in particular[27]. Simply increasing taxes without providing any other benefits or incentives for business to remain is a shallow solution and is more likely to be counter-productive. The same way a trader can't justify excessively high prices for a product that can be bought cheaper elsewhere, a government cannot simply increase the "price" to do business in the nation without offering a fair deal in return. Furthermore, the loss of opportunity for employment as well as a reduction in competition and goods and services offered, would further harm the very people that this policy aimed to help. By creating a disincentive for business, naturally, the number of businesses would decrease. The same applies to not just the corporations, but the individuals themselves. As alluded to throughout this manifesto, the power of incentives is not to be understated. It is important to highlight that imposing a higher cost on financial success would lead to people understanding they have less to gain by achieving those levels of success. Why would you work to achieve something where then an increasingly larger portion of it gets taken away in taxes? It would make more sense to someone achieving high levels of financial gain to move elsewhere in order to preserve or further expand their wealth in other places[28]. Taking with them the entrepreneurial skills that would otherwise have benefited the population of their domestic nation[29].

Alongside the retention of wealth argument, another factor to consider is the loss of domestic investment. By increasing taxes on the rich and large businesses, they are now left with less money to invest in capital. Money which would otherwise have been used to obtain better equipment, expand operations or hire more workers has now gone to the government to redistribute according to their own opinion on how best it would be spent. In other words, the money that would have been re-invested in the economy, has now been seized by the state to reallocate as they see fit. This revenue is now vastly dependent on whether the authorities are competent enough to adequately determine where this money should go rather than the market. Instead of this money being reinvested in a way that a more efficient organisation would benefit from, and in turn benefit others (more employment, better goods and services, etc.), it is likely to go into inefficient state programs that operate outside of traditional market forces. Neither adequately observing price signalling nor adapting to consumer demand. Alternatively, it may go towards funding wars that no one agrees with or be thrown at failing public organisations in the hope that more funding will solve all its problems. Instead of letting the market decide where to allocate resources based on demand and supply, the government decides where these should be used. All the while, chunks of this revenue is pocketed by politicians and bureaucrats in the process. The private firm being taxed, who initially made the profits, already proved its ability to allocate resources in such a way that meets the demands of the people. How does it then make sense to let the government gamble these earnings in non-market, uncompetitive enterprises that do not adhere to the laws of demand and supply? In a market environment, if a firm is allocating these resources inefficiently, then it itself will suffer the consequences and potentially fail, thus freeing up those resources for other more efficient businesses to manage. Whereas in a state redistribution system, it is the taxpayer who pays for the inefficiency of government enterprise. Although the intent may have been to help by redistributing to those in need, the actual outcomes may end up worse than intended. The market mechanism is what best redistributes wealth when government gets out of the way and makes it easier for competition to increase affordability and options for the people.

We should also consider that in reality, many of the high-income earners actually use tax avoidance schemes and spend money on "creative accounting" to get around paying these high rates. Other methods include them placing their money into tax protected bonds and other securities which would have otherwise been used in the economy. With convoluted tax systems, it is far easier for accountants hired by the richest in society to get around having to pay these rates by finding and exploiting both legal and illegal loopholes. This is not available to the poorer in society, since they cannot afford the fees to hire professionals specialising in this practice. On top of this, the experiment in excessively taxing the rich has already been tried. In 1921 the tax rate for earners of over $100,000 in the US was 73%. During this time, $700 million in tax revenue was raised, but only 30% of this class of earners paid taxes. But when this rate was steadily decreased to 24% by 1929, 65% paid and over $1 billion was collected in tax revenues[30]. Paradoxically, not only was more revenue raised with the lower tax rate, the coverage was also greater. Sowell explains that this was no mystery but was actually due to high-income earners being freer to use their earnings to reinvest into the economy rather than tax-exempt securities or other creative accounting methods. This reinvestment promoted greater output, employment and wages which in turn further raised the coverage since more income was available to be taxed despite the lower rate. What may have initially seemed obvious - that simply increase the tax rate will increase the tax revenue - the reality is that the relationship is actual an inverse one for the most part. Despite this, the tax burden still does not fall onto the lower classes of earners either within the US at least. Despite the progressive tax system and higher tax rates on the rich, it is still high-income earners who end up contributing the most to the overall tax revenue. This is because of the actual *effective* tax rate which takes into account the amount paid in taxes minus the amount given back in federal transfers. When looking at this, on average only the top 40% actually pay taxes more than they receive back from the government (if they receive anything at all)[31].

Under Azadism, a lower tax rate and simpler system overall would be employed initially. Since the role of state is far diminished, there would be less need for such a high tax revenue in the first place. Secondly, this would help retain wealthy individuals and businesses due to lowering costs on their success, making the nation more competitive in attracting wealth rather than to discourage it. By setting corporate taxes to zero, it would also help remove barriers to entry, as the cost of setting up and maintaining businesses is reduced. This all returns a net positive in terms of stimulation of the economy in forms such as: increasing employment, availability of goods and services, and promoting competition and innovation. As well as this, providing a simpler tax system by removing unnecessary taxes and progressive rates will help to remove the incentive to exploit loopholes and even increase the difficulty in finding them in the first place. If before you were being taxed 70% of your income, and by hiring an accountant (which would charge their own high fees) to, in theory, cut the cost you pay by half; why then would they do this if the tax rate is far below the 35% in the first place? Again, incentives must be considered in any tax policy suggested. Instead of the multi-tier tax brackets and vast variety of tax types, a flat tax on something like income would be implemented initially[32]. This tax rate would apply to all eligible equally. As discussed above, there is little concern about raising enough revenue with a lower rate, even though coverage is likely to increase anyway (and therefore also revenues). This simpler tax system makes it far more difficult to find loopholes and counteracts the incentive for the wealthy to use loopholes to begin with. For instance, the economist Milton Friedman calculated that under a flat tax system, the USA in 1962 could have raised the same amount of revenue with only a flat 23.5% tax rate[33]. At that time, the highest brackets went up to a mind-boggling 91%! Combine this with the small size of government and with most industries privatised, it is more likely for a national debt to transition into surpluses. These surpluses would then be used to further tweak the tax rate to let people keep their wealth rather than have the government squander it. Any excess should be handed straight back in full. This simpler and lower tax rate on the wealthy will also aid in attracting foreign investment, bringing with it increased opportunities for all in the nation.

With many of the inefficient and costly programmes the government provides removed, the private sector will take on most of these functions instead. By having lower costs to do business, it makes it easier for the people themselves to provide these solutions and compete with each other to create the best possible product or service, at the best possible price. The minimal tax rate, applied equally to everyone will fund the remaining state functions. However, Azadism being a dynamic philosophy, even this is temporary...

Tax is theft

The reader may recall the beginning of part three: the topic of Langar, Dasvandh and Choice. In there, it was made clear the immoral implications of a tax funded enterprise compared to a Dasvandh based one. For the reasons outlined there, an Azadist economy would eventually seek to phase out taxes all together in favour of voluntary donations. The responsibility is increasingly placed on the people themselves to fund the systems in place to protect them, even if there are "free-riders"[34]. Equally, if the government wants to continue to exist, then it must provide something of value to the people. This also maintains the balance of power between government and the people, as it gives the latter a greater ability to restrict the income of the government. On 15th February 2003, one of the largest protests in recorded history were held against the invasion of Iraq[35]. At the time it was clear to see public sentiment regarding this, however the politicians had the final say and went ahead anyway.

By having a donation based system, the government is in a much more reliant position. If these nations were operating under Azadism, then the people could have withheld the funding necessary to engage in that war[36]. The government would be financially handicapped to sustain any sort of campaign in that region. Whereas, with a tax-based approach, the people are extorted for their money regardless of whether they support the cause or not. By the very nature of taxes, each individual in a society is in part funding the indiscriminate drone strikes that murder both insurgents and children alike. Your earnings maintain the government monopolies on ineffective industries that would have otherwise innovated to find cures to dangerous diseases, or educated a population of innovators. You fund so-called wars on drugs, terror and poverty, that in reality tend to exacerbate these crucial issues further. If you refuse to participate, you yourself are labelled an *enemy of the state* and are kidnapped and thrown into a cage. Tax is fundamentally plunder. It is the acquisition of the people's property or hard work and labour in the form of money through force or the threat of force. Governments use the guise of "protection" in order to justify it, but how is this different to a Mafia? From murder to trafficking, if this manifesto listed the extent of the crimes of which government commits in the name of "protecting its citizens", this publication would become too voluminous. To recognise this reality is crucial.

Despite this, Azadism is not so radical in its approach that it is delusional about consequences. Doing away with all taxes overnight is likely to be devastating. Large changes such as these require time to phase out in stages. Many current systems of support provided by the state, however inefficient, could lead to disaster if removed too quickly for those that currently rely on them. Alternatives need time to arise and replace the state. Therefore, the tax reform process could follow this general order, in order to give time for the private sector to develop:

1. First, a flat tax rate system is implemented. All tax brackets are removed to leave one universal rate. Any other other types of tax are eliminated leaving only income tax or another alternative such as consumption or land value tax, since these could be argued to be far more appropriate to Azadist principles[37].

2. Then, over time the tax collection responsibility is devolved to smaller levels, beginning with individual states, and then further down to more local authority levels, perhaps individual cities and towns. These specific local governing units will be detailed in the final part, but for now, they would start being free to decrease the tax rate (but not increase), their revenue being gradually replaced by donation if required.

3. Eventually, each city or town is able to set their own rate, or none at all. This gives time for the private sector to develop and people's wealth to increase simultaneously. Those local units that refuse to reduce rates would initially be subject to market forces, where people could just move away, eventually restricting the local governments abilities. After a certain point, it would just be treated as theft, and the national security forces would be justified to put an end to this.

Ultimately the goal would be a taxless society, where even the state's functions could be replaced by competing private entities. Private courts and security services could replace the final state functions. However, this is a very long-term vision that may or may not be realised depending on the progress of the previous stages, and ultimately the will of the people. It is more reasonable to suggest that this be experimented with on smaller scales to begin with and then have the successful models exported to other localities if they wish to adopt it. Otherwise, if all residents of a particular area agree to pay into a fund pool voluntarily, acting as a "pseudo-tax" of sorts, then this is also acceptable[38]. And this already exists to some extent around the world with communes and other small communities. Since it is all voluntary participation, this is perfectly acceptable under an Azadist system.

This is not a foreign concept to Sikhi either. On giving the description of the ideal city, Begumpura, Bhagat Ravidas gives one of the qualities of the city to be free from taxes on goods.

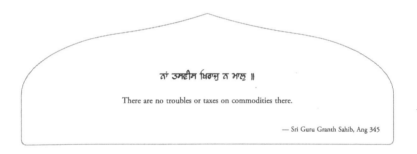

ਤਾਂ ਤਸਵੀਸ ਖਿਰਾਜੁ ਨ ਮਾਲੁ ॥

There are no troubles or taxes on commodities there.

— Sri Guru Granth Sahib, Ang 345

Alongside this, other qualities prescribed relate to social equality in terms of status and wealth and prosperity. The reader is encouraged to read the whole Shabad on Srigranth.org and explore the meaning of each word. Searching up the term "tax" on Gurbani search engines outputs a fairly clear perception of tax collectors too, often associated with Yama/Azrael, the messenger of death[39]. It is a shame how amongst the Sikh Sangat of today especially, attitudes towards taxes can often be supportive and treated as a preferential government activity. It just highlights the level of docility amongst the Panth today and the distilling of our Guru's teachings. Today we are happy being taxed and having the money we work for taken from us to fund the most unethical causes. Rare is it to hear any sort of outrage against this constant theft, from the Khalsa in particular. Instead the opposite is encouraged when seeing support for political parties that raise taxes and further increase the size of government. However, here is the response our Guru gave to the Hill Raje when they demanded taxes off him[40]:

ਸ੍ਰੀ ਕਲਗੀਧਰ ਗਰਜਿ ਕੈ ਮੇਘ ਮਾਨਿੰਦ ਬਲਿੰਦ । ਉੱਤਰ ਦਧੋ ਲਿਖਾਇ ਕਰਿ ਸੋਕ ਦੇਨਿ ਗਿਰ ਬ੍ਰਿੰਦ ।੧।

The Highest Plume-Wearing [Guru Gobind Singh], like thunder from giant clouds roared! The scribe began writing His response, which would strike pain in the hearts of the Hill Rajas.

ਚੌਪਈ ।
ਸੁਨੀਅਹਿ ਭੀਮਚੰਦ ਅਭਿਮਾਨੀ । ਸਾਭ ਰਾਜਨਿ ਸਨ ਦੇਹੁ ਬਖਾਨੀ ।

"Listen you cocky Bheemchand, convey this message to all of the other Kings as well.

ਹਮ ਤੇ ਦਾਮ ਚਹਹਿ ਜੋ ਲੈਬੇ । ਖੜਗ ਧਾਰ ਸੋਂ ਕਰਿ ਹੈ ਦੈਬੇ ।੨।

If you want to collect your tax I will give it you on the edge of my Kharag [sword].

ਤੋਮਰ ਤੀਰਨਿ ਸਾਂਗਨਿ ਅਨੀ । ਇਨ ਤੇ ਦੈ ਹੈ ਭੇਦੋ ਅਨੀ ।

On the tip of our spears and arrows we will give you your tax as we chop you into pieces.

ਸਲਖ ਤੁਫੰਗਨਿ ਬਰਖਾ ਗੁਲਕਾਨਿ । ਇਨ ਤੇ ਪਰਖਨ ਕਰਿ ਧਨ ਅਨਗਨ ।੩।

We will rain down your money with our bullets, come test the large amount of money we have set for you.

ਮੂਢ ਅਜਾਨ ਨ ਤੁਮ ਸਮ ਕੋਈ । ਚਹੋਂ ਦਰਬ ਲਿਹੁ ਸਨਮੁਖ ਹੋਈ ।

No one is as much an idiot and fool as you, if you want your money come face to face with me.

ਬੜੈ ਲੋਹ ਸੋਂ ਲੋਹ ਜੁਝਾਰੇ । ਲੇਹੁ ਪਰਖ ਤਬਿ ਦਾਮ ਕਰਾਰੇ ।੪।

Our warriors will ferociously clash iron with your iron, come then and test this money.

— Words of Sri Guru Gobind Singh, Gurpratap Suraj Prakash

However, again, Azadism recognises this as an ideal and not something immediately practical in this time. Instead this should be viewed as a direction to head towards or an attitude towards taxes that should be (re-) adopted, rather than something that needs to be removed overnight. Therefore, keeping in mind this compromise, the rest of this section will now focus on how the minimal taxes left could be used to help the disadvantaged as well as other methods to directly help the poor.

Inevitably, with competition there are winners and losers. Although, this manifesto has argued that this approach will lead to greater levels of innovation and prosperity as a whole, this does not discount the fact that this process is a gradual one. Along the way there is likely to be many who fail and enter periods of hardship. Those that inherently cannot take on the same opportunities due to a disability or whatever other reason are also at risk of falling through the cracks. How then does a state with a small government, which is largely restricted to only acting where the NAP is broken, provide the crucial safety nets for the disadvantaged or unlucky? The following will focus on the alternatives to extensive government intervention where freedom is not sacrificed in order to "help" the poor.

Universal Basic Income (UBI)

Although there are many different ideas on how to specifically implement this, in essence, UBI is paying every citizen of a country an income regardless of their current income or employment status. The primary advantage of this idea is that it provides a financial safety net for all citizens to fall back on. Whether someone has lost their job, business has failed or suffered an unexpected health condition, this will provide an income to maintain their basic human needs. As well as this, it may encourage people to take on the risk to opening their own businesses or pursue employment in occupations more in tune with their own personal interests.

What differentiates this from more common benefit systems is that with UBI you do not lose it when   you are offered employment. Current welfare systems suffer from a huge flaw known as the "welfare trap". If a person receives a job offer that's only just above the benefits they already get, in their mind, why would they abandon the free income that they already receive for no work, to go and work in a job they might not enjoy for minimal financial gain? In fact they may even consider themselves worse off if they take into account other non-monetary factors that raise their subjective *cost of working*. Increasing the amount of benefits will only worsen this situation further, as working will seem increasingly unattractive compared to staying on welfare. And we can't blame them. These mental calculations being made are only logical, since people tend to do what's best for them in their immediate situation. It is not because they are lazy or adverse to hard work, rather it is the way these welfare states are set up to increase the cost of working relative to staying on welfare. They are essentially trapped. UBI aims to mitigate this by maintaining their welfare income regardless of employment. Thereby, wages will be considered as an addition, on top of their income and not a replacement to it. In this way, they are always better off from working as the incentive to stay on benefits is diminished. If they decide to take on the risk, they could even establish their own enterprises, adding to the competition required for the functioning of a healthy free market. The fear of failing is also reduced, since they have the

UBI to fall back on. For those who are simply unable to work, UBI again provides a necessary support system.

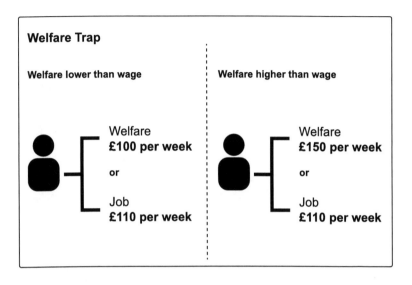

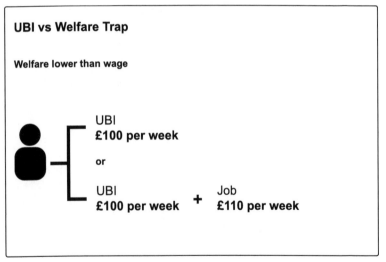

Negative Income Tax (NIT)

Although UBI is becoming an increasingly popular idea, an alternative popularised by the economist Milton Friedman, is the Negative Income Tax[41]. This aims to maintain the incentive to work whilst also providing the key social security benefit similar to that of an UBI. In this system, rather than a payment being given blindly to all citizens regardless of income, anyone earning below a certain *threshold income* will be subject to a *negative* tax rate. This means that rather than having to pay tax to the state, they receive a payment instead. The difference between their current income (including no income at all) and the national threshold income will be calculated and then, the NIT rate would be applied to this difference. Anyone earning over this threshold will be subject to regular positive tax rate.

The table below shows the current income and final income of three people. You can see here that someone earning nothing is still able to receive an income.

Example of the NIT applied to different income levels

Using threshold income of £30,000

Person	Current Income	Tax Rate (-/+)	Difference between threshold and current income	Difference with tax rate applied (deduction/ payable)	Total Income After Tax
A	£0	-50%	-£30,000	+£15,000	£15,000
B	£15,000	-50%	-£15,000	+£7,500	£22,500
C	£50,000	+13%	+£20,000	-£2,600	£47,400

It is important to note that with both UBI and NIT these payouts should only be enough to live off and not necessarily *thrive* off. Otherwise, there may develop a disincentive to work and again be stuck in a welfare trap. If someone loses their job or are unable to work, then this should be just enough to live off. This includes paying for their basic necessities and any insurances they may need. But crucially, it is their choice how they spend it. However, for most people this is unlikely to satisfy their lifestyle choices and so may be more encouraged to work and earn extra. If someone chooses to work in this scenario, the total income after tax will always increase the more you earn, thereby maintaining the incentive to work. Unlike UBI, the pay-outs are solely for the poorer in society, which means money is distributed to those that need it rather than it being paid out to the super-wealthy to whom it may be inconsequential anyway.

Another key advantage shared with UBI, is that people from the lowest financial backgrounds have a secure base from which to experiment in starting their own businesses. For example, Person A who currently earns nothing, may have a desire to become self-employed and not have to work under others at all. The NIT system allows them to take on this risk, as they have something to fall back on in case it goes wrong. Alternatively, the initial capital required may exceed the welfare income he gets, and so now he may be further encouraged to go work part-time at least, to earn some extra cash to help raise funds. What this has done is give him options as a means to engage in the market productively, as well as the safety in case he fails. Even if they fail, the lessons and experiences they get becomes invaluable. They are still free to try again, learning off their previous mistakes. If instead they wanted to detach entirely and devote themselves to do Tapasya, then they are in a perfectly comfortable position to do that also. This all falls in line with Azadist principles of freedom and options for people to live how they choose, provided the NAP is not broken.

Determining whether UBI or NIT is better is up for debate. Factors such as the costs of each method should be considered, as an NIT could be cheaper, however it could create perverse incentives for people to misreport their income. There are ways in which this can be mitigated, but for an Azadist economy, replacing current welfare states with a basic income based one initially seems a far better strategy to uplift the poor and protect the disadvantaged. Not only do these provide a basic safety net for people, but this may also revolutionise work-to-life balances in general. People may want to work less hours in shorter commitment contracts (part-time), and companies can offer more jobs to fill in the labour hours needed, thereby boosting employment in the economy. The current average of 30/40-hour work weeks may drop to 10/20-hour work weeks[42]. The mental health aspects also cannot be understated, as improvements related to stress were widely reported in previous UBI experiments[43].

However, a common argument against this is that this could take away the incentive for individuals to take on undesirable jobs that might be crucial for society to function. If you are paid regardless of whether you work or not, it is only reasonable that people, acting out in their own self-interest, avoid jobs they don't enjoy. In fact, it is also reasonable for people not to work at all and purely live off the basic income. Given a free market society, the laws of supply and demand may resolve this as it would mean a higher price must be paid for that work. Employers, seeing the shortage in the labour supply, would then have to increase the wages offered in order to create a greater incentive to take on those roles and compete for workers. What has essentially happened is that a new equilibrium price is reached for those roles, reflecting the new supply and demand in the labour market. The problem however may be that the return from the labour may not offset the cost of labour, meaning that some organisations will have to fail if consumers do not show enough demand for those goods or services. This is the market's way of communicating that certain enterprises are not worth the effort. In turn, resources are then freed up to encourage other entrepreneurs to invest in different ways or ventures.

This could also be assessed from another angle. With the rise of Artificial Intelligence and automation, many of these menial labour roles may inevitably be taken over by machines. If employers realise technology could be more efficient and cost-effective than hiring workers, then a basic income may be crucial for those who are replaced by them. By having this safety net, they could retrain and apply their skill-sets elsewhere. This should not be seen as a bad thing either. The nervousness felt now about current technological innovations mimics the industrial revolution. At that time, the horse carriage drivers must have also felt under threat by the invention of the engine and cars. However, it is difficult to argue against the insane amounts of progress that resulted from the advancement in that technology. By almost any metric we can observe, the world became better off as supply chains were streamlined, transport of goods and services became quicker and easier. Trade boomed, life expectancies rose alongside quality of life. Poverty, child mortality, death during child birth plummeted, all as a result of the innovations in technology and human ingenuity. New industries and opportunities would arise as technological advancement progresses. How many taxi driver jobs were there before the engine? Obviously none, however this was one of many industries that arose from it. The car may have also seemed like a complicated machine to master, but now it has integrated into society so deep it is often taken for granted. Similarly, with the age of the internet, many people who would have previously worked in factories and farms now work in offices, hotels, airports, etc, avoiding all of that back breaking work. Even with the corona virus pandemic, many sectors have become more open to the idea of working from home and offering more flexible work styles. Admittedly, there were many who may have suffered at the time of the industrial revolution who would not have had access to as many safety nets, if at all. Recognising that we as species may again be on the precipice for another revolution in technology due to things such as artificial intelligence, blockchains, green technology etc. It is crucial that adequate measures are put in place *now* to help protect those who will inevitably be affected. Basic income may be one way of providing this.

Bringing this back into the roadmap for an Azadist state, the government would initially combine NIT with a flat tax rate in the beginning, in order to best attract wealth, prosperity and competition whilst providing necessary social security[44]. Government programs would be entirely replaced by a NIT. For those nations who are transitioning to an Azadist model, they may do this by reallocating the budget dedicated to their current welfare systems to this one gradually. Eventually this would phase out all uncompetitive, state-owned monopolies in the welfare sector. Over time, the tax revenues collected by the rest of society will go towards funding this instead. A modification to the traditional NIT system would be that in an Azadist state, people born with disabilities would be offered a higher NIT rate to help offset the potential lack of equal opportunity due to their circumstances. There is likely going to be extra costs involved with their situation (medical insurance, equipment, lack of employment etc.), and so to help offset this, slightly more could be offered.

A drawback with this welfare system, however, is that it still involves taxes. It also requires at least some level of government bureaucracy to manage this distribution. Albeit far less than current social security programmes and welfare states, it is a risk nonetheless and so over time even this should be phased out in accordance with Azadism's tendency to reduce government intervention as much as possible. Devolving this responsibility onto more local levels may help this at first, but innovations in blockchain technology especially may be leveraged to drastically change the approach to this entirely, thereby removing much of the bureaucracy. Eventually, as taxes are phased out, NIT must also. Instead, if people want to keep this, then it would rely on donations and become voluntary. This is to maintain the principles of freedom and thus moving away from any sort of "forced" philanthropy. Therefore further responsibility is placed on the people themselves to help each other through their own compassion and not coercion. However, this is all long term and an Azadist state should not completely phase out basic income until enough of the population passes an agreed level of prosperity.

"The problem of poverty is money..."

— *Milton Friedman*[45]

Minimum Wages

Minimum wage laws are perhaps one of the most detrimental policies currently implemented that keeps the poor in poverty and removes their opportunity to progress. This statement may sound oxymoronic initially since you would assume that imposing a minimum amount that a company must pay its employees should increase the income of low earners. However, there are two angles to this that are often overlooked.

The first is from the business's perspective. By enforcing this policy, what is essentially happening is that by law, the government is making it illegal to hire workers below this rate. This means that the government is artificially increasing the cost of labour as well as increasing the cost of doing business. Whilst larger or more developed companies (maybe with already higher paid staff) can easily cope, smaller businesses are the ones taking the hit. Using an example of a restaurant, if a dishwasher is only producing £5 per hour worth of output, but must be paid £10 per hour, then the business simply cannot afford to keep them, and certainly can't afford to hire more. Now maybe the chef is forced to fulfil that role instead, which in turn may put more pressure on them, reducing their productivity and time spent doing the specialised role they were hired for. This all puts extra strain on the business. With higher minimum wage rates, it makes it even harder for people to expand or to set up their own businesses in the first place. Also, by increasing the price of labour, businesses are often left with no choice but to raise prices to compensate for these increased costs. Not only does this make small businesses more uncompetitive compared to large ones (who are able to afford the higher costs anyway), but it also further harms the poor by making goods and services more expensive and thereby reducing their already diminished purchasing power. Greater reliance is then placed on the larger corporations as their prices may not rise as much in comparison. From the business perspective, minimum wages protect the large corporations and reduces their competition by filtering out the small businesses from the market. If the desire is to increase reliance on large corporations, whilst simultaneously destroying opportunity for smaller competition and new entrepreneurs, then increasing minimum wages is the correct policy to do so.

The second perspective revolves around missed opportunity. If less businesses can afford to hire workers, then the amount of employment opportunity decreases[46]. Low skilled labour especially now have less options. Without minimum wage restrictions, they could have at least worked for a low wage, learned valuable skills on the job and gained vital experience to progress further. But with high minimum wages, often that first step on the job ladder is missed entirely. Work experience is often critical for being able to progress, but instead under these laws they gain nothing; neither income nor experience. Often it is young people in these positions, and by pricing them out of the labour market early in life as well as encouraging them to take on massive university loans puts many in financially poor positions with reduced opportunity. For other demographics from impoverished backgrounds, these laws have taken away any opportunity for them to earn at all and so must rely on the state provided welfare systems. It is even harder to start your own business and grow it too due to the greater barriers to entry mentioned above. As well as this, the rise in automation will also need to be considered. By making human labour more expensive, alternatives become more attractive to firms seeking to minimise costs. Minimum wage laws remove much of the bargaining power for low-skilled workers and condemns them to welfare.

As mentioned earlier, the safety net should be from the NIT instead, which does not operate at the expense of the ease of doing business. This way, small companies are not forced to provide a living wage since the NIT should be able to cover that instead. This is not the entrepreneur's responsibility, it is initially the states' under an Azadist framework (and then later to the people themselves). Under Azadism, NIT would provide the liveable income, and so employers and employees are free to negotiate contracts that are mutually beneficial for both parties. This allows for a market price of labour to be developed tailored for each circumstance. With costs of setting up and doing business reduced, naturally it would correspond to a rise in the number of businesses being able to be set up, and therefore employment opportunities also increase. This translates to more competition for that labour. If one business offers a wage too low and working conditions too poor, then the potential worker has ample choice to find work elsewhere that's more suitable for them. Now, both the employer and the employee are protected and left to flourish in a freer and fairer environment. On one side businesses compete to secure workers by offering suitable pay and standards to attract them as well as giving the poor and low skilled more opportunities to find work. On the other side, businesses are more able to reduce costs and offer wages more in line with the natural value of that labour. This in turn, allows for easier expansion of operations and the cost savings translate into better prices to consumers. This is a win-win situation.

Private Charity & Civil Society

Inevitably, there will always be some people who will suffer hard times and fall through the cracks. By removing barriers to entry, increasing competition and affordable options through free markets, naturally a society would develop that maximises prosperity. However, even after all the efforts mentioned so far, for those who still fall into hardship, the final webbing in the social safety net of an Azadist society is *private charities*. All those who may need extra help can use these institutions and people can donate money to these charities through their own choice if they are passionate about the cause.

In addition, private charities would have a better incentive to solve problems rather than perpetuate them, since their income revenue is based on performance rather than taxes. If a charity were not solving a problem, then why would people continue to donate? The same goes for any service in a competitive market environment. If a charity was not performing well, then people would donate to a competing one instead. Whereas a state department solving the same issues has no competition nor has any incentive to be efficient since their costs are paid for by the taxpayer. Efficiency is important here especially since it saves more resources that can be used to help more people. So if the government programs are performing sub-optimally, then the rest are left with very few options depending on how restrictive the regime is. Instead, what tends to happen is that excuses such as "lack of funding" may be raised, where the state then simply throws more of the taxpayer's money at the department, expecting that simply funding an ineffective venture would magically solve its problems.

Michael Tanner, senior fellow at the CATO institute exposes the fallacy of government "aid" further. When he appeared before the US Congress, he testified that only 30% of funds designated for the purposes of charity through entitlement programs in the US actually went to the intended recipients. The other 70% went into the pockets of administrators. Comparing this 30% with the 82% private charities manage to get to the ones in need, the ridiculousness of the situation becomes apparent. Imagine a charity that only passed on 30% of donations to the target recipient. Who in their right minds would donate to them if there were alternatives that reached over 80%? Especially considering that the government has no comparable fund-raising expenditure, since this is extorted through taxes anyway. Private charity on average spend 8% on raising funds, and the final 10% goes to pay administration costs (such as salaries)[47]. That is the difference between government and private charity. It cannot be repeated enough - these are the reasons why Azadism is so against granting government monopolies over industries in an economy, especially in welfare.

Furthermore, the role of private charities falls under something called "Civil Society". This refers to all non-state-owned institutions and organisations involved in making up a community. These are essentially private efforts but function primarily to satisfy social requirements rather than profit maximisation. These include institutions such as religious bodies, community centres and even family. The historical role of civil society must not be understated, as for much of history it was institutions like these that provided for those who suffered in society. When undergoing any sort of difficulty, the first port of call would be those around you. Family, friends, neighbours, and then maybe onto religious institutions, societies, associations, and charities. None of this requires government monopolies funded through forced taxation.

Removing the state as the only option for these people frees up the ability of the community to solve these issues themselves. The state can only provide any sort of support using taxpayer's money anyway, which is acquired through force, and then spent by the state in the way of their choosing. How would a person stealing from someone else in order to give to another be reflected positively in any moral system? Especially when that person pockets a portion of this money, and then is unable to effectively translate what's left into sustainable ways of helping others anyway. Under Azadism, it is considered better to remove the middle man that is the public sector and help directly. Or if we want to use an intermediary then a system in which we are free to choose who may best fulfil this function is the best course of action. By having a government in the way of this process, not only does one condemn their own personal freedom in how to help others, but they also hamper the ability to give effective support to the needy. Competing charities, who have an incentive to look for solutions are far better suited at this role than government is under Azadist thinking. This way gives options to the people in order to choose where they think their own money will be most useful, as well as give them the choice to actual go out and help themselves. Getting rid of taxation in this process, would also naturally leave them with more money to commit to these causes as well. The case for *forced* charity through state theft is weak in comparison.

This section has outlined the overall social security safety net for people in an Azadist society. For Azadists, a whole new mindset is adopted in the attitudes we hold towards government as a care giver. Instead of acting like children we break the paternal relationship we have granted government as a society. For the Khalsa, we already have our father as Dhan Sri Guru Gobind Singh, and our mother Aad Shakti Mata Sahib Devan. Why should we place governments on the same level? Whether it be in the form of civil society, private charities, or individuals themselves, the state needs not to provide any more safety net than already mentioned in terms of NIT initially. This helps mitigate the risk of the government becoming too relied upon and as a result grow in power and influence. As discussed in the previous section, a government too large, covering too many roles is a detriment to the quality of life in a nation. People should realise that the real power is with them as individual, private actors, separate from the state, and as a result should take responsibility themselves for the betterment of their own lives and those around them. An Azadist tax system is designed as a compromise between the coercive nature of tax and maintaining the right to choose how people spend their money, all whilst the state can provide some level of security in the beginning whilst the private sector (us the people) builds up to take over. Eventually in the long-term plan of an Azadist state, even the tax system should be phased out in favour of a voluntary donation for the remaining government services if required. This is the balance between prosperity and safety, whilst trending towards greater freedom and prosperity. It must be stressed that the phasing out of these services must be gradual and in the long term. The situation must be constantly monitored and assessed to ensure maximum safety by having necessary alternatives in place for those that currently rely on government services.

"Clearly we are doing something wrong. Throwing money at the problem has neither reduced poverty nor made the poor self-sufficient. It is time to re-evaluate our approach to fighting poverty. We should focus less on making poverty more comfortable and more on creating the prosperity that will get people out of poverty"

— *Michael Tanner*

The emphasis on equal opportunity over equal outcomes forms a major part of Azadism. Promoting the former rather than the latter by getting government out of markets, removing its ability to create barriers to entry and establishing unfair competition by granting or becoming monopolies themselves, naturally leads to a situation where anyone is able to work to achieve their own goals. By allowing opportunity to be absent of barriers, leads to prosperity and would therefore mean that very few in a society would even need to be on welfare at all[48]. When comparing the top 10 most charitable nations, we can see on average just over 50% of the populations of these nations give to charity[49]. Following this trend, with lower taxes, and potentially more disposable income, people would have more funds available to spend on these causes if needed. Azadism requires a removal of the NIT system only when enough of the population's average income rises above the initial threshold level. This gives time for these charity organisations to grow, so as the nation transitions from a developing to a developed one, the necessary private institutions would already be in place and ready.

To conclude this section, a repeated emphasis must be put on the people themselves to take action. Look to our Gurus for supreme guidance here. The Gurus did not take money from the Sangat to give more taxes to the Mughals to provide charity. They instead set up Langars to feed the world themselves. Instead of coercing people, they encouraged all those to donate Dasvandh through their own choice. Instead of relying on the state to provide, they themselves took up the responsibility. Similarly, Azadism pushes people to take personal responsibility, do not rely on the state. It should be every Sikh's desire to conduct Seva using their own hands, why pass this on to a state monopoly with dubious morals and a track record of greed, corruption and lies? In modern times there are many who have embodied this and have applied the example of the Guru. Bhagat Puran Singh didn't wait around for any government. He took the initiative himself and set up Pinagalwara alongside other like-minded people[50]. Similarly, Ravi Singh from Khalsa Aid banded together those around him as a private individual to provide support in regions hit by war and natural disasters[51]. Greater freedom should be given to people like these, who are the true embodiment of Azadist principles in private charity. And perhaps, one the greatest inspirations comes from the

Sakhi of Bhai Kanhaiya, who gave water to dying soldiers of both friendly and enemies forces equally. As a result, they were commended by Guru Gobind Singh themselves as understanding the true essence of Sikhi[52].

As promised earlier at the end of the section on *Langar, Dasvandh and Choice,* please consider this final Sakhi to conclude this discussion. During the times of Guru Nanak, there existed a public worker for the Mughals named Ganggu Bhagu. Through extortion and dubious means, he raised funds to conduct a Śrāddha ritual aimed at venerating his dead ancestors. As part of this he also offered free food, paid for through the funds he stole. Maharaj was passing by at the time and was also invited to partake in the offerings, however Guru Ji refused after inquiring about the situation. The following Shabad was then revealed in response[53]:

ਜੇ ਮੋਹਾਕਾ ਘਰੁ ਮੁਹੈ ਘਰੁ ਮੁਹਿ ਪਿਤਰੀ ਦੇਇ ॥

The thief robs a house, and offers the stolen goods to his ancestors.

ਅਗੈ ਵਸਤੁ ਸਿਞਾਣੀਐ ਪਿਤਰੀ ਚੋਰ ਕਰੇਇ ॥

In the world hereafter, this is recognized, and his ancestors are considered thieves as well.

ਵਢੀਅਹਿ ਹਥ ਦਲਾਲ ਕੇ ਮੁਸਫੀ ਏਹ ਕਰੇਇ ॥

The hands of the go-between are cut off; this is the Lord's justice.

ਨਾਨਕ ਅਗੈ ਸੋ ਮਿਲੈ ਜਿ ਖਟੇ ਘਾਲੇ ਦੇਇ ॥੧॥

O Nanak, in the world hereafter, that alone is received, which one gives to the needy from his own earnings and labour. ||1||

— Sri Guru Granth Sahib, Ang 472

Just as Bhagu was taught this lesson by the Guru, we ourselves must also heed this message. No matter how pure the intent, and whatever charitable cause it is aimed at, the entire effort is invalidated when the funds used are produced through coercion of other people's resources. Only that is considered acceptable where something is done out of your own earnings and labour. Forcible redistribution of wealth is immoral under these circumstances. Instead, Azadism looks at incentive-based solutions that encourage charity and personal responsibility in helping those in need. This attitude of stealing from certain groups in order to satisfy the needs of others is inherently flawed. The only exception to this is if those individuals we take from are themselves thieves and you are returning what is rightfully owned by another. Merely being wealthy does not automatically mean they achieved their wealth through exploitation. In a free-market society, where the roles of the public and private sectors are completely independent of one another, the only way someone can accumulate wealth and riches is by providing a product or service that others are freely willing to pay for. If government officials like Bhagu (and Bhago from earlier) are stealing and exploiting, then it is justified to put an end to this in order to maintain the NAP. A thief is one who takes what isn't theirs. Just because it is politicians and the state doing the taking, it does not exempt them from moral judgement. If any other private actor did what the government does, they would be arrested and jailed. It is only under the threat of force - the fact that government is able to kill or kidnap you so easily, does this plundering through tax continue to exist or was even set up in the first place. In return for protection, we are persuaded to give in and accept the status quo. However, we forget to consider that often the greatest threat to a citizenry is not other citizens, it is instead their own governments.

V

The Role of Government

Limiting Government in Size, Scope and Power

Tyranny and Democide

History has repeatedly shown the failures of relying on the state to provide for its citizens. The Sikh Panth in particular has suffered greatly under tyrannical regimes, that may be on paper secular and democratic, but in reality are divisive and catered towards their own elitist desires of power and control. By pitting one group against the other, the people are divided and squabble amongst themselves, and in this way the rulers maintain power. However, the counter to this may be that the people simply need to elect a "good" leader, one who will be just and compassionate. And this may seem true initially, and perhaps even obvious. History has had its examples of venerated rulers, from Marcus Aurelius to Maharaja Ranjit Singh. Cyrus the "Great" was so revered by the Jews, that he was even praised in their scripture as a messiah, the only non-Jew to be given the title. From our own Ithiaas, Raja Janak in particular is a famous example. A king who attained enlightenment and conquered desire and attachment. The ideal of "philosopher kings" espoused by Plato has indeed been realised throughout history. But they were rare. An exception not the rule, lasting as only oases in a vast desert of tyranny and oppression. Aurelius was the last of what Niccolo Machiavelli called the "Five Good Emperors", as after his death the Roman empire fell into times of great hardship and civil war with the infamous "Year of the Five Emperors". Maharaja Ranjit Singh invested heavily in arts and culture as well as implemented many beneficial reforms. But this also ultimately fell apart due to betrayal from within his court. Dying without a clear successor led to internal strife, which was further exploited by the British to destroy the empire entirely. Even after the death of Cyrus, the Achaemenid Persian Empire, although largely prosperous, eventually led to rulers growing up in luxury and becoming weaker and weaker, until Sikandar from Macedonia steam-rolled them and sent the Emperor Darius into hiding in his own lands[1]. The message here being that having a system that so heavily relies on the competency and benevolence of the ruler is inherently flawed. As soon as they go, so does the prosperity that relied upon them, and ultimately it is the people who suffer. To rely on the long term compassion of a government in Kaljug is not only naive, but can often be disastrous.

There is no "right man for the right job" since the job itself is wrong. No one individual, or small group should hold a monopoly on force by centralising power into a select few. Aiming to elect a group that will adequately represent an entire society is not only unrealistic, but dangerous. No exclusive group of people are capable of managing the vast diversity of societies, the complexity of which gives rise to so many different needs and wants. To suggest that a singular entity can successfully manage the trillions of transactions that occur daily in the modern world is not only wrong but ludicrous[2]. Even a ruler with good intentions, seeing the limited resources of which he controls, may try to prioritise by pandering towards one group but in the process excludes another. Ways in which this has been dealt with has often resulted in tragic consequences for a population. In order to maintain supreme control, ruling classes have engaged in heinous acts by first "simplifying" the systems they control. By eradicating diversity and freedom of expression, they aim to establish a population that is homogeneous. Having a population that thinks and acts the same is far easier to manage, and for any tyrant this becomes a more desirable route after realising how complex managing a state really is. They have no shame in manipulating the truth and applying labels such as *"enemies of state"* to weed out opposition. Monopolising and nationalising media they control the narrative and make terrorists out of freedom fighters. Using religion as a weapon they turn their genocides into holy wars and praise is given to murderers, rapists and paedophiles. Through this, they destroy any opposition and criticism of their actions believing that they know best, or it is for the "greater good". Creating a public enemy of an individual or group, they engineer a population to murder themselves. This is not conjecture, it is history. The 1984 genocide followed this formula, by demonising Sikhs and turning those who fought for Dharam into terrorists via a variety of methods[3]. Even today the narratives around the genocide is rife with misinformation and propaganda. It is a fallacy to think that the Indian state has progressed since then. Hindu Nationalism is once again on the rise. Organisations like the RSS are openly performing a cultural genocide through their assault on linguistic and religious freedom. Not surprisingly, Hitler's Mein Kampf is a best-seller amongst India's right wing[4]. It was for the purity and greater good of the German race, Hitler had also justified his actions. He did not think he was the one in the wrong. Censoring alternative opinions, and ostracising opponents becomes a necessity in their mind. By having unchecked power at the top, the leaders determine what is just, and are willing to commit the worst terrors to uphold it.

The Soviet Union is a prime example of authoritarianism gone wrong. Vladimir Lenin, after leading the Bolshevik revolution in Russia, deposed the Czar and began to nationalise industries. Rejecting free trade and private property, he and his party enforced a policy which permitted the state to take control of factories and businesses so that they could centrally plan where resources should go. Neither could anyone lease or own land, or hire workers. Instead labour was controlled and people were assigned roles given by the state. Critically, farmers in particular were targeted by having any excess crops above anything needed to feed themselves confiscated and given to the government to determine how it would be rationed. Initially food was sold at reduced fixed prices, with the government being the sole purchaser[5].

Inevitably, due to these fixed prices being far lower than the ordinary natural price determined by market forces, the incentive to farm diminished as there was no profit motive. The farmers were less driven to produce extra crops, since they knew all the hard work they put in would not be rewarded as it would just be confiscated anyway[6]. As a result crop production plummeted alongside other industrial outputs. Cities and towns in the USSR were brought to the verge of famine. The farmers worked out ways around these restrictive policies and established a so-called "black market"[7]. Peasants known as "bagmen" filled their grain into sacks to travel into the cities and sell directly to the people. When Lenin found out about this, he issued his infamous "Hanging Order", which ordered them to be publicly hanged to soak fear in the populace[8].

Unsurprisingly, this further acted as a disincentive for labour in the agricultural sector leading to widespread food shortages, plunging the population into a famine. Millions died as a result of this mismanagement of the economy. Lenin, realising his mistake, then drafted what was now known as the "New Economic Policy" (NEP) in order to free up the economy for private enterprises based on a profit motive to be established at a limited level[9]. However, he made it clear to maintain this under strict state control.

This allowed the economy to develop somewhat as a result, which further highlights the importance of the economic freedom of which Azadism is based on. Even the black markets acted as a lifeline for those in the cities. However, due to the state still having so much control over so many aspects of the economy, the USSR naturally fell back into crisis when the next autocrat took charge.

After World War One, the region of Ukraine was split up into various territories of which the majority was ceded to Bolshevik Russia. Lenin was succeeded by Joseph Stalin who put an end to the NEP and began to institute new reforms to bolster industrialisation[10]. To achieve this, Stalin introduced the first of a series of "Five-Year Plans", which became common amongst later nations aiming to emulate the Soviet central planning models[11]. Unfortunately, despite its initial boost in employment and industrial output, this too inevitably failed. The peasants became increasingly oppressed, in particular a class known as the "Kulaks" who were allegedly wealthier. The state began by raising tax rates and setting more demanding performance quotas for the production of crops. Eventually, they expropriated property just as Lenin did, and deported thousands of families to other areas of the USSR. Stalin then adopted a model of collectivising the farms to further reduce the power of the farmers and peasant classes. This was a step further than Lenin had originally implemented by confiscating produce, as it meant that individuals were no longer permitted to even owning their own farms and land. Instead they were forced to join large collective farms owned by the state but managed by multiple families[12]. The state would then pay them a salary depending on how best they met quotas. Naturally, unwilling to part with their private property and generational homes and lands, the peasantry revolted by killing their cattle and destroying necessary machinery. Stalin cracked down harshly in return and sent millions of them to Gulags. With much of the labour supply diminished alongside equipment and livestock, output dropped. However, Stalin still forcibly requisitioned what remained and exported much of it abroad, simultaneously starving the population. Despite Ukrainian exports for wheat rising to its highest rates ever at the time, Ukraine itself and other areas of the USSR had entered another famine. The Soviet state security forces and secret police used to go house to house to collected the dead. Peasants caught "stealing" food were executed on the spot, and as the death toll rose countless were thrown into mass graves. One story tells of a situation in which they even took people alive but too weak to resist, so to save time on having to collect their bodies later. They too were thrown into the mass graves and buried alive. The sheer brutality of these events got to such a level and people were in such a desperate state that cannibalism emerged as parents began to eat their own children[13].

The Soviet Union was an extreme example of totalitarian regimes, however not an exception. Their particular brand of ideology and methods were imitated by Mao in China, resulting in the deaths of tens of millions of people[14]. Cambodia under Pol Pot was also inspired by them, killing between 13-30% of the entire population[15]. Even today in North Korea, the Korean people suffer from central planning, living under strict state control. Brutal punishments are handed out to anyone who resists, one particularly gruelling example is the *yeon-jwa-je* - "Guilt by association". This includes punishing entire families, even imprisoning three generations worth of members in prison camps. Under hellish conditions, adults, elderly and children alike are forced to work from 5:30AM to midnight. They are often starved, beaten and tortured to death[16]. This is not history, this is happening right now.

Countless are the examples of state exerting its power in this way throughout history. Our own Ithiaas is full of them. From Guru Arjan Dev Ji, attaining Shaheedi under the Mughal emperor Jahangir to the genocide of 1984 at the hands of the Indian state, the Panth is no stranger to tyranny. During Auranga's reign, the authoritarian Mughal state also degraded religious freedoms, imposing discriminatory tax rates based of religion in the form of the Jizya. Hindu merchants were forced to pay higher tax rates than Muslim merchants. Prominent Hindu temples were destroyed, such as the Kesava Deo (believed to be the birthplace of Krishna) which was demolished and a Mosque reconstructed on top. Due to the increasing oppression, several revolts had arisen and were suppressed by the Emperor's forces. A religious sect known as the Satnamis also rebelled against this tyranny however the state forces completely eradicated their entire order[17]. All unorthodox Muslims including Shiites and Sufis were also persecuted for their alternative interpretations of Islam. Kashmiri Pandits also feeling the wrath pleaded to Guru Tegh Bahadur to help them avoid the state mandate to convert to Islam or die. By confronting Auranga and challenging the Emperor to convert him to Islam instead, the Guru was tortured for weeks before finally attaining martyrdom themselves, alongside his companions Bhai Dayal Das, Bhai Mati Das and Bhai Sati Das. Never giving in to the forced conversion, they secured the religious freedoms of the oppressed.

This all culminated into the formation of the Khalsa under Guru Gobind Singh, expanding on the militaristic institution of the Akal Sena established by his grandfather, Guru Hargobind Sahib. The Guru, seeing the overarching oppression by the state, aimed to liberate the people by giving them sovereignty over their own lives, away from state coercion. Seeing the timidity of the common man, and building upon the work of his predecessors, he transformed them into saint-soldiers. Weapons became the articles of faith, and using them to wage war against tyranny became the new religion.

ਚੁ ਕਾਰ ਅਜ਼ ਹਮਹ ਹੀਲਤੇ ਦਰ ਗੁਜ਼ਸ਼ਤ ॥

When all other methods are exhausted

ਹਲਾਲ ਅਸਤੁ ਬੁਰਦਨ ਬ ਸ਼ਮਸ਼ੇਰ ਦਸਤ ॥੨੨॥

To pick up the sword is permissible ||22||

— Sri Guru Gobind Singh, Zafarnamah

Jai Bhagouti

As eluded to throughout this manifesto, the role of an Azadist government is reduced to only a few critical areas initially to begin with, from which power is then dissolved further. These are:

1. National Defence
2. Policing
3. Justice system
4. Tax Administration

This takes the economic power out of a select group of people and into the hands of the ordinary population participating in private, mutually agreed transactions. The government has no say in how individuals negotiate their own contracts. As seen earlier, this may take the form of getting rid of any minimum wage laws, that violate the freedom of negotiations between employee and employers, or another example is removing any restrictions on the types of goods and services sold (as long as it does not violate the NAP). A desirable consequence of the latter example is the purchase of weapons. This is encouraged to ensure the ability of the population to defend themselves against tyrannical governments, either domestic or foreign. A well-armed populous, with weaponry sufficiently permeated throughout society, sets up a fail-safe or a last line of defence from the tyranny previously discussed. Guru Gobind Singh also makes this ideology abundantly clear through numerous examples throughout their Gurbani and Ithiaas[18]:

ਬਿਨਾ ਸਸਤ੍ਰ ਕੇਸੰ ਨਰੰ ਭੇਡ ਜਾਨੋ । ਗਹੇ ਕਾਨ ਤਾਕੋ ਕਿਤੈ ਲੈ ਸਿਧਾਨੋ ।੯੮।

Without long hair [kesh] and weapons a man is a sheep, grabbed by their ear they can be dragged anywhere. [98]

ਇਹੈ ਮੋਰ ਆਗਿਆ ਸੁਨੋ ਹੈ ਪਿਆਰੇ । ਬਿਨਾ ਤੇਗ ਕੇਸੰ ਦਿਵੋ ਨ ਦਿਦਾਰੇ ।

This is my command listen my beloved ones, without a sword or long hair [kesh] do not come to see me.

— Words of Sri Guru Gobind Singh, Gurbilas Patshahi Dasvi

Maharaj makes it absolutely clear the state of those who are without any means of defending themselves. Those who are unarmed are susceptible to any sort of oppression and tyranny. They can be so easily herded like sheep, and consequently butchered like cattle also. Kesh is another symbol representative of freedom, since in those times long unshorn hair was a symbol of sovereignty in both temporal and spiritual terms, as well as belonging to the Kshatriya class. Similarly, around the world intact hair was a common motif for freedom and expression of one's traditions and culture; so much so that often the first thing slavers and conquerors would do is cut off the hair of the enslaved. Long hair, being associated with many other warrior cultures throughout history, the Guru is also emphasising the importance to remain free and defiant in the face of tyrants, by implanting warrior/royal ethos into the hearts and minds of the average man. A popular reasoning as to why the Khalsa adopted the Dastar is also to represent an open defiance to the state mandates at the time that only royalty or select classes were permitted to wear a turban. Not only did the Singhs defy this, but wore tall turbans, using two cloths hence Du(two) Mala(cloth). Kshatriyas have always historically been the caste of kings in India, and so when the Guru establishes the order of the Khalsa, he gave the opportunity for the ordinary man to become a king, regardless of their social status, wealth and other arbitrary conditions.

ਛਤ੍ਰੀ ਕੋ ਪੂਤ ਹੋ ਬਾਮ੍ਹਨ ਕੋ ਨਹਿ ਕੈ ਤਪੁ ਆਵਤ ਹੈ ਜੁ ਕਰੋ ॥

I am the son of a Kshatriya and not of a Brahmin who may instruct for performing severe austerities

— Sri Dasam Granth, Ang 549

As private, non-state actors, the Gurus themselves established and maintained their own sovereignty. Erecting the Akal Bunga (Takht), Guru Hargobind Sahib challenged the states authority by building its platform higher than permitted by a royal edict decreeing that only the Emperor could sit on a raised platform of over three feet. The Guru wearing two swords, a Kalgi and other insignia of royalty, regularly sat on this raised platform and mirrored the duties of a king as a private individual in an act of open defiance to state authority[19]. Later, his predecessor Guru Gobind Singh would complete this transition of taking away state power, by blessing all Sikhs with the status of Kings with the birth of the Khalsa. The Khalsa Panth became the next successor to the Guru alongside the Shri Guru Granth Sahib.

ਤੂੰ ਕੋ ਮੈ ਸ਼ੇਰ ਬਨਾਉਂ ਰਾਜਨ ਕੇ ਸੰਗ ਰੰਕ ਲੜਾਉਂ

I will turn Jackals into Lions, I will make the servants fight the Kings

ਭੂਪ ਗਰੀਬਨ ਕੋ ਕਹਲਾਉਂ ਚਿੜੀਉਂ ਸੇ ਮੈ ਬਾਜ ਤੜਾਉਂ

I will turn poor into Rich, I will make sparrows break hawks

ਸਵਾ ਲਾਖ ਸੇ ਏਕ ਲੜਾਉਂ ਤਬੈ ਗੋਬਿੰਦ ਸਿੰਘ ਨਾਮ ਕਹਾਉਂ॥

I will make 1 fight 125,000, then my name shall be Gobind Singh.

— Oral tradition, attributed to Guru Gobind Singh

The hawks being the tyrannical rulers of the time, the corrupt authoritarian state[20]. Seeing the oppression levied upon the people of India, and the atrocities committed by the Mughal government, the Guru crafted a militia of his own from the ordinary people to combat this. Maharaj embedded the warrior ethos of the Kshatriya into the saintly nature of the Sikhs crafted over nine lifetimes of the preceding Gurus. Through this, the ordinary people were uplifted and turned into the status of warriors and kings. Again, all in the effort to maintain freedom and individual liberty against the state.

Tyrants, in the examples of the previous subsection, recognised the danger of an armed population and so acted swiftly to ban them. The Soviets confiscated guns and enacted strict gun control laws after taking power, which was similarly replicated by other parties with similar tendencies for central planning and overarching state control. A particularly egregious example being the Nazi party of Germany under Hitler, who after removing most of his opposition, only then relaxed restrictions (especially for fellow Nazis), except for the Jews who were strictly repressed from gun ownership and thrown into concentration camps[21]. Ironically the US National Rifle Association (NRA) used a similar tactic in 1967 when they supported a bill to restrict open carry of firearms in California despite their heavy pro-gun stance. This was an effort to restrict the Black Panther party at the time from their activism and highlighted the double standard the NRA held when Black people sought to express the same rights to guns[22].

During the British Raj in India, restrictions on weapons were also strictly enforced. Slowly in the Panth itself, Shastar began to lose its once highly respected position as post-colonial distortions of Sikhi seeped into their minds. Where before Sarups of Guru Granth Sahib were rarer and less accessible, Shastar Prakash was common in Gurudwaras and memorials to Shaheeds instead, acting as the point to prostrate towards and do Parikrama around[23]. One of the few groups left that preserved these martial ideals were the Nihang Singhs. However, many of these warriors attained martyrdom fighting the British alongside their Jathedar, Akali Baba Hanuman Singh. The few survivors retreated south to Hazur Sahib, away from much of the British influence and hence why even today they maintain many of the original

Kshatriya traditions of our Gurus and the Singhs, such as Jhatka and Shikaar[24]. After this period, a "shoot-on-sight" policy was enacted, that wherever a Nihang Singh was seen, they were to be killed on site and shot twice in the head since they were known to carry on fighting even after the first shot to the head[25]. This extermination did much to suppress the warrior ethos of the Sikh Panth as a whole. Even the Kirpan wasn't spared as the size gradually decreased, eventually forcing a Hukamnama to be issued by the head Granthi at Hazur Sahib at the time, Akali Hazura Singh, decreeing that a Kirpan to be worn with a Kamarkassa should be no less than one foot in length. Giani Sher Singh, a prominent scholar and Granthi[26], explained the tragic consequences of the disarmament attitudes of the Panth. During the 1984 genocide, those families who kept the Guru's Shastardhari Maryada alive were the ones who survived and those who didn't were brutally murdered with their children being burnt alive on the streets, and mothers and daughters having their honour taken from them.

This is the importance of keeping armed, and being unrestricted in doing so. It is to protect oneself and others when the state follows the footsteps of the tyranny before them, thus continuing the age-old tradition of *democide*. The population themselves must recognise and accept responsibility for their own sovereignty and to keep the freedom that an Azadist state is built upon. Democide is not an exception, it is an inevitability of authoritarianism. It is only ever a matter of *when* not if. For these reasons, Azadism does away with any sort of gun-control, confiscation or selective rights to weapons, by granting the right to own weapons unrestricted to all citizens.

The Founding Fathers of the United States, similarly recognising these factors in their own constitution codified a similar sentiment through the Second Amendment, ensuring the right for its citizens to bear arms:

> *"A well regulated Militia, being necessary to the security of a free State, the right of the people to keep and bear Arms, shall not be infringed."*

A well-armed populace acts as a fail-safe against oppression. Therefore, it is of the utmost importance that the trade of weapons are not restricted. People themselves need to take responsibility for maintaining their own freedoms, and constantly check that the government does not increase power and influence. The use of weapons against those taking away freedom is morally legitimate even if state laws declare it illegal[27]. If the state or anyone attempts to relinquish the right to arms then the private individual should give a response equal to what King Leonidas of Sparta gave to the Persians when asked to surrender weapons. Freedom can equally be seen as a natural state, instead of something that is acquired necessarily. To achieve freedom is to remove barriers that inhibit it. Shastar being one of the most crucial components in order to do so. It becomes abundantly clear why the Guru worships weapons, seeing that they are the vehicle to freedom[28].

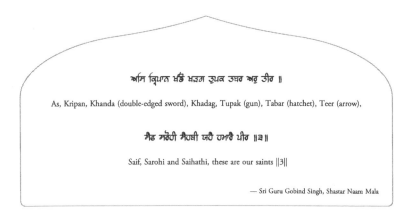

ਅਸ ਕ੍ਰਿਪਾਨ ਖੰਡੋ ਖੜਗ ਤੁਪਕ ਤਬਰ ਅਰੁ ਤੀਰ ॥

As, Kripan, Khanda (double-edged sword), Khadag, Tupak (gun), Tabar (hatchet), Teer (arrow),

ਸੈਫ ਸਰੋਹੀ ਸੈਹਥੀ ਯਹੈ ਹਮਾਰੈ ਪੀਰ ॥੩॥

Saif, Sarohi and Saihathi, these are our saints ||3||

— Sri Guru Gobind Singh, Shastar Naam Mala

The horrors of what happens when the state becomes the sole monopoly on force is why Azadism despises forced authoritarianism in all its forms. It completely rejects ideologies and actions that aim to give greater power to the state, economically or politically, since it recognises the vast suffering that ensues when it goes wrong. It is not blinded by naivete to simply expect that by electing someone new that somehow this time "it will be different". The Mughals replaced the Lodis, Lenin was brought to power after deposing the Czar and Hitler too inherited the status of Führer via democratic means. Simply replacing one centrally planned state with another, one authoritarian regime with the next, is not the solution. The problem is the state itself. Too much power concentrated in too few people.

When the Guru makes reference to securing *Raaj,* is he referring to just another state, or political party or regime? Or is he referring to the people themselves, private individuals taking the right to rule their own lives in their own hands. Azadism interprets this as the latter. Real Khalsa Raaj is wherever a Singh plants his foot.

> *Satguru had conferred sovereignty on the Khalsa Panth,*
> *As well as on each individual Singh of that fraternity.*
> *Wherever a Singh sets his foot and settles on earth,*
> *He establishes his own self-reliant/autonomous sovereignty.*
> — *Rattan Singh Bhangu, Prachin Panth Prakash*

True Raaj is not the ability to coerce and command others to do your bidding. It is the power to take sovereignty over your own mind, body and spirit as well as allowing others to be free to do so too.

ਆਈ ਪੰਥੀ ਸਗਲ ਜਮਾਤੀ ਮਨਿ ਜੀਤੈ ਜਗੁ ਜੀਤੁ ॥

See the brotherhood of all mankind as the highest order of Yogis; conquer your own mind, and conquer the world.

— Sri Guru Granth Sahib, Jap Ji Sahib

Whenever the state oversteps its role, it must be the people who take back this power into their own hands; weapons in all their forms are the tools to do this. To be Shastardhari is not merely opening an old sword museum in your house full of rusty blades, it is the constant striving to do battle, and the preparedness that comes with training - to be *Tyaar bar Tyaar.* Weapons are not just limited to the medieval equipment of the old times, even the Guru's advanced their arsenals through adopting firearms and even inventing their own cannons[29]. Furthermore, to fight battles was not just limited to the physical fight either, just as the Guru killed Aurunga through the Zafarnamah, similarly the freedom must be upheld for the people to criticize their government without censorship. They can also write and inspire policy change through non-physical violence. Whatever means of doing battle is chosen, the battle must be fought constantly to limit the power of the state so to avoid tyranny and oppression.

The Khalsa especially should realise this responsibility as it has done so throughout its history. Pandering towards pro-state ideas and granting greater powers to government is not only antithetical to Azadism, but Khalsa Mat in general. This manifesto is just one effort to combat the growing sentiment in the Panth of supporting nationalisation and other anti-private policy. The vast majority of this comes from ignorance of what policies actually do in terms of freedom. The mark of a society that is declining into totalitarianism is the relinquishing of power from the people and into the hands of a few. This may be done in many ways, as shown throughout this manifesto. Censorship, nationalisation of industry, increased regulations and licences, but perhaps most importantly, gun control. So that, when these authoritarian systems eventually fall into barbarity, the people have nowhere to turn to, and no means of resistance. Don't expect the world to step in. Who stepped in when people of the Soviet Union was starving or thrown into Gulags? Who gave aid to the Native Americans when they were invaded and enslaved? What about when the Jews were persecuted under Hitler? Where was the world in the countless massacres and genocides throughout history? Any action that was taken was too late. These are not just restricted to history. Who is stepping in now to save the Uyghurs, Rohingya and North Koreans? Or the Palestinians and Israeli people who are caught in the middle of two *governments* warring with each other? These things can only exist when the people themselves hand over their collective power to a small group of "representatives", forgetting that a government, a king, an emperor, a dictator was meant to be a servant to the people and not the other way around.

Democracy

To avoid these tyrannical situations from arising in the first place, it is imperative that the government is structured in such a way as to mitigate this risk. Most of this risk has already been alleviated through the nature of an Azadist government being one of minimal intervention and restricted to the roles mentioned previously. This should be formalised into a constitution of sorts, and held in the highest regard by the people themselves. The rules in that constitution should be held almost as sacred as religious articles to ensure its adherence. As well as this, the armed population should be always ready to defend this constitution less they risk suffering the consequences of authoritarianism. It is therefore the peoples own responsibility to maintain this first and foremost. Any changes are likely to be insidious, but once this document is established, it should not be changed in any way to add further power to the government. The current stance of Azadism already allows for the maximum participation possible. A society can only be classed as Azadist if, at most, the state is responsible for military, police, courts and taxes. Anything that privatises this even more is just more Azaad, until you get to full privatisation, a.k.a Azaadi. Ways in which this could materialise is adapting the tax collection and redistribution system to be managed by blockchain technologies, AI or other ways to reduce the bureaucracy involved.

Another recommendation for the well functioning of an Azadist nation is to do away with a democracy in the form of simply giving everyone a vote. However, firstly, it is unlikely that there will be many issues to vote on anyway since the market itself is responsible for its own economic decisions such as trade deals, minimum wages, welfare or any other policy decision a politician would usually make for them. The Athenians were one of the earliest civilisations who actively worked against the establishment of an authoritarian system. They had learned the lessons of giving too much power to a ruling elite and knew full well the consequences of having freedoms eroded[30]. Through the establishment of democracy, they aimed to disseminate power amongst the population. Although, an improvement, there were still some serious weaknesses present in the Athenian experiment. What inevitably arose was a system in which those vying for power would use any manner of misleading speech to simply appear better than opponents, rather than having any actual rational policies. The voting populace, who were not educated in the nuance of certain matters, would simply pick the candidate who had the more convincing argument, but not necessarily the rational one. The word given to such people was "demagogues", who were masters of rhetoric rather than reason[31]. Plato describes an argument presented by his teacher Socrates in his work *'Gorgias'* on this matter, where he gave an example of a court trial that had indicted a doctor. The accuser being a cook that baked meats and treats, and the jury being a group of young boys. The cook would be able to easily sway the jury's opinion by highlighting the scary-looking instruments of the doctor, bitter-tasting potions and other practices, claiming that he on the other hand offers sweets. Amongst a population who do not know any better, it is unlikely the doctor could make any substantial counter argument[32]. Socrates further expands on this in Plato's *"The Republic",* using his famous allegory of the "Ship of Fools". You wouldn't let just anyone manage the sailing of a ship and all the other roles involved. Instead, you would want those skilled and educated in these matters to be responsible. The same logic is then extrapolated onto voting and deciding how a nation should be managed. Seeing the inherent flaws of democracy, Socrates advocated that voting should be equally recognised as a skill that requires time and effort to hone. It is not simply a birthright[33].

Potential improvements therefore could be that voting rights should be reserved only to those who have a proven ability to think rationally about the arguments presented and have shown that they have indeed thought about their vote. Just like a driving test is required before obtaining a license, similarly, a test could be set up ahead of a vote that those wishing to participate must pass. If the citizens recognise the importance of being educated enough to vote, then they may demand this education in the market. Those that decide not to or are unable to put in the time and effort required to pass this test will simply be barred from voting. The test should be careful to avoid bias and mainly stick to questions ascertaining whether people simply know what certain terminology even means. Those creating these tests should obviously not be allowed to vote. This is all to reduce the effect of demagoguery, whereby politicians manipulate voters by gaining sympathy through rhetorical arguments, where they push policies that are counter-productive but sound nice in order to gain power. The reality is that many people are not educated enough to be able to make an informed decision, and so the rest of the population shouldn't suffer as a result. But what happens if a single class of people are actively restricted from this education? Who decides what questions to put in this test in the first place? Does having more minds truly solve the complexity of certain decisions? There are many *stupid-clever* people. And there are many who are truly intelligent but still make the wrong decisions[34]. By introducing barriers to entry for political representation, do we really reduce the risk of demagoguery, or do we give demagogues a smaller group to influence?

Azadism sees democracy as a form of mob rule. It is the majority deciding on the behalf of all. Minorities will inevitably have their interest sidelined for the benefit of the majority. This goes completely against the principles of freedom and the NAP on which Azadism stands. The only area in which it may be acceptable is privately. Private democracies can exist if each individual agrees to have their personal will triumphed over by the majority vote. There is nothing wrong with this, and it already exists in social groups everywhere for situations as mundane as deciding where to go hiking with friends. Similarly, private autocrats can exist too as long as adherence to their laws are voluntary to participate in. This is what most businesses are like, which also have autocratic structures and company policy. They are almost states within a state, with a king at the top (CEO) and all his ministers (managers) and subjects (employees of various roles) underneath. However, the difference here is that each member can voluntarily choose to leave at any time. If people do not want to seek employment in that structure, then nothing is stopping them from trying different ways of organisational management such as worker co-ops, provided that they are all still free to leave and join at will. It just so happens that human beings seem to tend towards hierarchical structures, and autocratic systems seem to get things done quicker as there is less deliberation, for better or worse[35]. As long as this all occurs privately there is no problem with voluntary authoritarianism. In fact, this is what we Sikhs see the Guru as - a private "monarch", transcending the royalty of the state. Each Sikh is a subject to this authority voluntarily and abides by this monarch's dictates completely of their own volition[36]. No matter how much in majority, a non-voluntary democracy on a state level in which one group decides on the behalf of another, is always unjust in principle if the other group is forced to comply according to Azadism.

Similarly, the founding fathers of the US realised these issues too, and instead established a constitutional republic in which the rule of law would always take precedence[37]. In fact, the word democracy was never used in the constitution or the declaration of independence. They feared the same thing that Socrates had in the sense that a *direct* democracy will eventually end up in tyranny, as the people will inevitably elect in a dictator after some time. This is exactly what happened in Germany with the rise of Hitler who was also elected democratically. Although a republic is also technically democratic, it introduces a series of measures to ensure the constitution is held in the highest regard, and that a series of representatives are elected to make decisions on the behalf of those they represent. The problem with the early American system, however, was the barring of groups such as women and Black people from engaging with any of this. The founding fathers themselves followed along with the thousands of years old tradition of slavery, despite its monstrous social implications as well as economic drawbacks[38]. But even today, the way in which representation is determined has become completely broken due to a practice known as "gerrymandering". Elected groups are able to redraw the boundaries in which representatives are chosen so that certain parties are favoured over others, even if they had less votes overall[39]. Combine this with the sheer amount of things that the government is responsible for, you get a system arguably as bad as the very direct democracy they were hoping to avoid.

The comprehensive outline of how exactly an Azadist system would function politically goes outside of the scope of this particular manifesto, and may be expanded upon in later publications. However, for now, these are some of the things to consider when thinking about this topic. Choosing between monarchy, direct democracy, republic or any other form of government may be the wrong approach entirely. What has been proposed throughout this manifesto, is a system in which decisions are made by the people that only affect themselves and those who freely consent to be affected by them.

Instead of pushing for any system that aims to decide on the behalf of others, Azadism inherently takes away this ability and places importance in maintaining freedom whilst actively protecting against those behaviours that breach the freedom of others. In other words, only that system of governance is truly acceptable that upholds the NAP. Any government that adopts Azadism as an economic policy is by default condemning itself to become gradually more limited, more privatised and more decentralised. But how would a nation starting from scratch do this? How could an existing government restructure itself to abide by the tenets of Azadism? The next section will explore one hypothetical form of government that is based on many of the principles advocated so far.

Raaj Karega Khalsa

To reiterate, the role of a government in an Azadist society would be solely for defence and protection against entities aiming to destroy personal freedom and property. It aims to ensure the free functioning of the markets and mutual transactions that occur within its nation's borders. The enemies of an Azadist state are ones who disregard the NAP and it is the government's only duty to protect against them. However, you may be wondering that if government as an entity is so incompetent and destructive, why then give some of the most crucial functions required for the well-being of a society to them also? Why have a government at all? The reason is that people have Stockholm syndrome. After so many thousands of years of being ruled and abused in various forms of authoritarianism, it has seeped into our collective consciousness that we need a government. We have learned to love our abuser. The idea of free-markets is relatively new and is still widely misunderstood or not even in common awareness[40]. To get to a stage where a society becomes open to these ideas, a gradual step-by-step process must be undertaken in order to successfully transition safely. The roadmap laid out in the section about taxes is a good place to start. With this, you can begin to see real-world implementations of limiting government power. This section will now outline a hypothetical framework in which this could exist.

To start, we will begin with the nature of those individuals in government. Firstly they should adhere to a philosophy of non-duality. Seeing all things as simply an expression of what is fundamentally unified, their definition for God should be the very quality of existence itself. God, and existence, should become synonymous in understanding. Through this, all humanity is considered equal and as a result worthy of the same love, protection and respect they expect for themselves. No one is higher and no one is lower. Nothing is to be feared nor hated since all of it is a manifestation of themselves. This should not just be believed, but felt and internalised through daily remembrance of these facts. Through meditation and singing of the praises of existence, these are acceptable methods of remembrance. On top of these things, they must adhere to a strict discipline of abandoning the vices of lust, anger, greed, attachment, and pride. This is measured by the level of their involvement in charitable acts of kindness and devotion to the methods of remembrance. Additionally, their efforts in studying existence and time spent teaching others is also worthy of consideration. They must actively seek to understand the nature of the self as illusory, merely a *story* we tell ourselves[41]. It is a heuristic that is only necessary for playing along with this play of energy and matter. Understanding that objective reality acts as a base layer for which a subjective layer of beliefs, systems of thought, religions etc. are placed on top of it in order to help understand it, or at least navigate it. The only way of observing objectivity is to remove the "you" from the equation[42]. Until that happens, these individuals need only to show an active striving for that state of being. This way, the opinions, lifestyles and beliefs of others are respected as just different subjective mappings of existence. This is the spiritual philosophy necessary for the functioning of a limited government, that strives to uphold human freedom.

Secondly, the means by which they interact in this world is to protect against those who desire to destroy freedom. Therefore, it is essential that those individuals should be skilled in violence but also restrained in when to use it. They should be immersed in both combat and spirituality, so that even when they use violence it is only ever in the interest of protecting freedoms and the lives of the innocent. Fighting out of hatred is not only shunned but illogical. How can you hate when you realise that all are simply a bundle of atoms travelling in this universe at different trajectories than your own bundle? If all is you, and you are everything, what is there left to hate? Compassion, righteousness and duty, willpower and determination should be paramount virtues for members of this government if they want to remain in power. Balancing both spiritual and temporal aspects, they should be saint-soldiers. However critically, they should be saints first and then soldiers, always valuing the spiritual above the temporal. In order to help ensure these things, personal sacrifices should be made by these individuals to radically change their appearances to constantly act as an outward reminder of the responsibilities they hold. They should keep their hair long, to represent the long hair of warrior-kings and spiritual masters of the past, such as Yogis, Sadhus and Sidhs. They should then care for this hair and uphold a level of hygiene of both thought and action, symbolised by a wooden comb. Another reminder of this should be an iron bangle worn on the wrists. Cotton drawers with a knot to secure it should also be worn to ensure a message of purity and reluctance to delving into uncontrollable desires and vices. Lastly, a weapon must become another limb of their body, never parting with it as to be always armed and ready to fight against injustice and tyranny. What a coincidence, something like this already exists! Thankfully, none of this needs to be set up from scratch as the Guru has already provided an organisation of this nature. Azadism thus suggests placing the *Khalsa* as the "government" of an Azadist nation.

It is now even more important that the initiation into the Khalsa via Khande di Pahul is re-formalised into a serious, professional event. Just as it was during Guru's time, and throughout the Khalsa's history. The Khalsa government needs to ensure that this is now a formal introduction into the Khalsa army and not just some ritual with no commitment. This doesn't mean that every Amritdhari Sikh has to become a battlefield soldier, but instead by partaking in Khande di Pahul, it initiates a Khalsa into a government job - a servant of the people. A Khalsa Singh or Kaur would have the option to do Seva as a soldier, police, court official or tax administrator. By keeping Rehit it guarantees at least some level of commitment to upholding the ideals of an Azadist government of which the principles are similarly derived. By abandoning previous names, castes, and other social commitments, they must take on a new identity as part of the Khalsa.

The specifics on how the Khalsa may be structured goes beyond the scope of this particular publication since it is mainly focused on the economics. Nevertheless, some principles of Azadist economics can be applied here too in order to let us begin to think about the ideal way to manage the risk of giving one organisation a monopoly on force. One of these principles that has been the bedrock of Azadism is competition and decentralisation. Applying this in this setting, the Khalsa could be arranged once again as Misls, as they were before the time of Maharaja Ranjit Singh. Each Misl would have their own leader, elected in their own way with a set of Rehit Maryade specific to each regiment. A Khalsa who is recently initiated can then assess which Misl they would like to join and apply (each may have their own requirements or tests), or alternatively, the Misls themselves could administer Khande di Pahul and recruit that way. The Misls who stray too far from Khalsa principles would naturally get less Khalsa joining them, and if they become anti-Khalsa, the other Misls are then free to disband and destroy that unit through negotiation or battle[43]. This ensures that the wider Khalsa Panth always has supreme power as a collective, which corresponds with the mandate from the Guru to give the Khalsa sovereignty.

The Guru then handed over his double-edged dagger to the Banda Singh,
Which he accepted and wore around his person as an armour.
Feeling enraged at the loss of their legitimate right of being Guru's heirs,
The Khalsa Singhs stripped Banda Singh of Guru's armour. (11)

Chaupai : As (the) stripped Banda Singh complained to the Guru (about the Singh's act),
The Guru went into peels of laughter with immense joy.
The Guru remarked that with Singh's forcible possession of their legitimate right,
His mission of empowering the Khalsa Panth has been fulfilled. (12)

— *Rattan Singh Bhangu, Prachin Panth Prakash*

If the entire "Khalsa" Misls become corrupted over time then the people themselves, who were free to hold Shastar also, now have the duty to overthrow the government and re-establish constitutional law and a new set of Khalsa Misls. Any Khalsa is free to join, leave and even set up their own Misl just like private businesses in an economy. Their success is determined by how well they perform their role in protecting the population. If a Misl is failing at their role, another one is free to come in to replace them. All the people need to do is transfer their Dasvandh to another Misl[44]. This is where Azadism's conception of the Misl system differs from the historic one. Instead of imposing a "Rakhi", or protection tax on the people, they instead offer their services more like a business. Each Misl then competes for "customers" the same way businesses do in a free-market. In fact, in the same area, multiple Misls could co-exist for different groups of customers within the same locality, the same way how multiple supermarkets exist to meet the needs of different consumers. Some Misls could specialise in courts, others in policing for example. This competitive aspect allows for a system of checks and balances, so that there is a constant struggle and incentive to maintain the Azadist principles. Eventually, these Misls would be more akin to private security/military contractors as society becomes more Azaad.

Reasonable concern may be raised in regards to Misls fighting each other, just as they did when this was tried previously in our history. However, the following few things should be considered. The Khalsa is by nature violent. Violence itself is not a moral issue, only when and how to use violence is. If the incentives are managed in a way where the protection of the citizenry is put first, then any sort of violence on behalf of Misls will largely be restricted to fighting each other as a means to out-compete one another to achieve this goal. This is especially the case when taxes are removed in place for an optional Dasvandh, where the competition is now to appease the needs of the people in return for payment to the Misl. The same way businesses have to compete to win over customers by offering better products and services, the Misls needs to provide the best possible assurance in its ability to protect and serve. Otherwise, the people can just withdraw funding and pick another Misl. The "infighting" also avoids the issue of tyrannical oppression, as has been seen with so many dictatorships of the past, since now the government is too preoccupied with itself. If each Misl is too busy fighting each other (and even this fighting is over the favour of the people), then the risk of democide is drastically reduced[45]. The Misls would therefore keep each other in check and leave the people alone. Additionally, war is a highly resource intensive and destructive activity. It's often a huge waste of time, effort and life that could have been used far more productively elsewhere. In a system of Misls who are all competing with each other to provide the best service possible, it is illogical to engage in such behaviour as it leaves all parties involved worse off. There are less funds, less strength, and above all, less trust. The people, or customers of these services, can look at the state of these entities and come to a conclusion that they are no longer fit for purpose and choose a Misl that did not get involved with any of this. Alternatively, it is also possible that the victorious Misl could have proven its ability as a stronger, more able service provider than the one that lost. This is completely fine too, it's up to the people to decide what they want for themselves.

If a Misl decides to extort the populace instead, then two counter-balances exist with this system. The first is other Misls. Either the people themselves could call for aid, or other Misls could see and act directly as they would be their constitutional duty to prevent a violation of the NAP. These Misls would have an incentive to liberate the oppressed due to the fact that this would be seen as their Khalsa Dharam, and also because it would reflect positively on their Misl and grant them a better reputation. This is then extremely useful for future employment. The second component is the people themselves. If the population successfully heeded the messages of the previous section regarding staying Shastardhari, then they would be well equipped to secure their own freedom if the need arises. Through the very fact that everyone is armed, every house becomes a fortress and each family is an army[46]. This acts as a huge deterrent to anyone seeking to take your private property and your liberty. If a society rejects Shastar, then what else do they expect? They will be led by the ear like sheep to the slaughterhouses, becoming just another story in the history of democide. Even if outnumbered and all odds are against you, is it not better to die fighting with weapons in hand?

ਦੇਹ ਸਿਵਾ ਬਰ ਮੋਹਿ ਇਹੈ ਸੁਭ ਕਰਮਨ ਤੇ ਕਬਹੂੰ ਨ ਟਰੋਂ ॥

O Shiva, give me this boon that I may never hesitate from performing good actions

ਨ ਡਰੋਂ ਅਰਿ ਸੋਂ ਜਬ ਜਾਇ ਲਰੋਂ ਨਿਸਚੈ ਕਰਿ ਅਪੁਨੀ ਜੀਤ ਕਰੋਂ ॥

I may not fear the enemy, when I go to fight and assuredly I may become victorious.

ਅਰੁ ਸਿਖ ਹੌਂ ਆਪਨੇ ਹੀ ਮਨ ਕੌ ਇਹ ਲਾਲਚ ਹਉ ਗੁਨ ਤਉ ਉਚਰੋਂ ॥

And I may give this instruction to my mind and have this tempotration that I may ever utter Thy Praises.

ਜਬ ਆਵ ਕੀ ਅਉਧ ਨਿਦਾਨ ਬਨੈ ਅਤਿ ਹੀ ਰਨ ਮੈ ਤਬ ਜੂਝ ਮਰੋਂ ॥੨੩੧॥

When the end of my life comes, then I may die fighting in the battlefield ||231||

— Sri Dasam Granth Sahib

Nonetheless, these are the extremes of possibility. In actuality, it is highly unlikely this would be commonplace due to the economic infeasibility alone. The market would filter out the undesirable traits as Misls compete to appease the will of the people. Two markets run simultaneously, one being the Khalsa collective joining and leaving Misls depending on the adherence to Sikh principles, and the other being the people themselves voluntarily devoting funds to those Misls that best meets their needs. This ensures that the government remain as Sevaks, not predators.

ਖਾਲਸਾ ਸੋਇ ਜੋ ਕਰੇ ਨਿਤ ਜੰਗ ॥

Khalsa is the one who is [always/daily/regularly] engages in [spiritual/political] warfare

— Bhai Nand Lal, Tankahnama

As Sikhs, we shouldn't be too adverse to the idea of the Khalsa fighting each other either. It is the Khalsa's nature to do battle, both physically and mentally. If anything it's healthy and keeps all the Misls in line and self-regulating, as well as disciplined and focused. This doesn't necessarily mean that they have to aimlessly kill one another all the time, but instead there are many ways to do battle. Level headed Misldhars looking to emulate the examples of the Guru could similarly engage in duels as was once done against Mughal commanders, thus avoiding needless bloodshed of each other's forces. Alternatively, no physical engagement is required when Misls can join together in a regular Sarbat Khalsa to discuss matters and engage in debate. The Sarbat Khalsa gatherings could also provide a platform to present new ideas and innovations, and help facilitate the Azadist transitions to higher degrees of economic Azaadi. If desired, competitions and contests could also be held here to settle disputes or just to display specific "unique selling points" of each Misl. Loh Mushti and Guru Angad Dev Ji inspired wrestling matches could be just some of these ways[47].

A decentralised force like this, with an armed population, only adds to the security of the nation as a whole. It becomes almost impossible for foreign invaders to take over. Consider the recent defeat of the US in Afghanistan. Although there was foreign support, the Taliban had followed the same model to defeat the Soviets[48]. The reason for their success lies in the fact that the Taliban are not a centralised force. It is a collection of thousands of tribes united against a common enemy. By employing guerilla warfare tactics they mastered the *art of war* in this way[49]. To fight them is to fight a thousand nations in one. A similar situation existed in Ancient Greece, made up of multiple city-states, each running their own experiments in statecraft. However, when faced with an external threat, they then unified to defeat the Persians whilst remaining as individual, independent entities. The original Khalsa Misls were similar. Made up of twelve Misls, they successfully worked together to dispel both the Mughals and the Afghans from the region of Punjab. Only when the Misl system was abandoned for a monarchy under Maharaja Ranjit Singh did Punjab then collapse to foreign enemies.

As Sikhs, we have a romanticised view of Maharaja Ranjit Singh's empire, and despite all the positives that came out of it, it was still a fundamentally flawed system doomed to fail at some point. The high state investment into arts, education and religion only existed due to the benevolence of the ruler, and therefore all this flourishing relied on him. Once the Maharaja died, so did his empire. Even without the betrayals, there was no guarantee that his successors would match his reputation, and history is littered with examples of the failures of the progeny of great kings. This shows the unpredictability of having a single ruling class in terms of their attitudes towards their people. This was also seen during the Guru's time as some Mughal rulers befriended the Guru's, whereas others showed hostility. And this bipolar nature isn't even restricted to one descendant to the next. Some of the same Emperors who earlier in their lives went on hunting expeditions with the Guru, later betrayed them. Increasing, or centralising, the power and influence of a government only maximises the severity of the destruction they can commit. Why would it seem reasonable to gamble lives on whether a ruler turns out benevolent or tyrannical? A sure way to mitigate this risk is to take the power away from the government in the first place. A government that is for the people and by the people should be considered a servant of the people. To prevent a servant from stabbing the master, take away their knife. In the same way, if we don't want our governments to oppress us, we should take away their capacity to do so. This involves reducing the size of government so it's only responsible for a few limited things.

Even during the time of the Sikh empire, the Khalsa under Akali Phoola Singh were the counterweight to Ranjit Singh, and they could even be argued to hold more influence than the Maharaja himself. Even the Singh's in the Khalsa armies would completely disregard any status of Ranjit Singh, and actively made sure he would know this. All this shows that the Khalsa has always been opposed to the state, even if the ruler was a Sikh. From very the inception of Sikhi, authoritarianism has been opposed, whether this was against Brahmanism, Mughals, Afghanis, British, or even in modern India. Although, worthy of some exploration is the claim that despite its flaws, monarchy can still be more desirable than a bureaucratic democracy. Hans-Hermann Hoppe is a political theorist and economist who makes the argument that a king and his family have more of an incentive to comply with the people's will lest they risk political instability and ultimately an overthrowing of their entire dynasty. Therefore, it was often the king's own family who would kill and/or replace him, in order to secure the dynasty. This is perhaps why the particular monarchy under Ranjit Singh worked well for its time since Akali Phula Singh as a representative of the Khalsa was able to keep the Raja in check. Compare this with a democracy, it is far more difficult to kill off who is responsible, since who exactly is responsible? Even the death of a prime minister or president is very unlikely to destabilise the entire system to the point of collapse. However, it must be stated that both are still seen as deficient methods of governance by Hoppe, and the sole purpose of his exploration was to show the lesser of two evils[50].

ਹਰਣਾਂ ਬਾਜਾਂ ਤੇ ਸਿਕਦਾਰਾਂ ਏਨਾ ਪੜਿਆ ਨਾਉ ॥

Deer, falcons and government officials are known to be trained and clever.

ਫਾਂਧੀ ਲਗੀ ਜਾਤਿ ਫਹਾਇਨਿ ਅਗੈ ਨਾਹੀ ਥਾਉ ॥

When the trap is set, they trap their own kind; hereafter they will find no place of rest.

ਸੋ ਪੜਿਆ ਸੋ ਪੰਡਿਤੁ ਬੀਨਾ ਜਿਨ੍ਹੀ ਕਮਾਣਾ ਨਾਉ ॥

He alone is learned and wise, and he alone is a scholar, who practices the Name.

ਪਹਿਲੋ ਦੇ ਜੜ ਅੰਦਰਿ ਜੰਮੈ ਤਾ ਉਪਰਿ ਹੋਵੈ ਛਾਂਉ ॥

First, the tree puts down its roots, and then it spreads out its shade above.

ਰਾਜੇ ਸੀਹ ਮੁਕਦਮ ਕੁਤੇ ॥

The kings are tigers, and their officials are dogs;

ਜਾਇ ਜਗਾਇਨ੍ਹਿ ਬੈਠੇ ਸੁਤੇ ॥

they go out and awaken the sleeping people to harass them.

ਚਾਕਰ ਨਹਦਾ ਪਾਇਨ੍ਹਿ ਘਾਉ ॥

The public servants inflict wounds with their nails.

ਰਤੁ ਪਿਤੁ ਕੁਤਿਹੋ ਚਟਿ ਜਾਹੁ ॥

The dogs lick up the blood that is spilled.

ਜਿਥੈ ਜੀਆਂ ਹੋਸੀ ਸਾਰ ॥

But there, in the Court of the Lord, all beings will be judged.

ਨਕੀ ਵਢੀ ਲਾਇਤਬਾਰ ॥੨॥

Those who have violated the people's trust will be disgraced; their noses will be cut off. ||2||

— Sri Guru Granth Sahib, Ang 1288

In describing the state of Kaljug, Guru Nanak in Raag Malhar[51] sings of the oppression applied by the kings and their accomplices. If any sort of Khalsa Raj was to be established, it must bear in mind these facts. It should actively work towards maintaining freedom in society and stray away from any form of non-voluntary authoritarianism.

Further to this, Azadism does not seek to emulate the past but instead learn from it. Simply trying to recreate medieval Indian feudalism because of nostalgia is irresponsible. Instead, Azadism seeks to use the lessons from history and the present to establish a system that is based on Sikh principles as well as the latest developments in the study of statecraft. This approach is inspired by Guru Gobind Singh themselves, who not only studied the best available literature on the subject for his time but also ordered his Khalsa to similarly study governance and politics[52]. Realising the corruption that has arisen within his own Sikh institutions (set up by previous Gurus) he abolished the Manji system and punished the Masands. The sovereignty given to the Khalsa also gives it the ability to change and adapt according to the time. The Khalsa, being the representation of the Guru alongside the Guru Granth Sahib, also later changed the structure of the army under Nawab Kapur Singh, and the subsequent adoption of guerilla tactics. By placing the Khalsa as the caretakers of an Azadist system, the role of the Khalsa is best realised as the protectors of human freedom and flourishing.

Goal of Government and Enforcing Ethics

What is the overall purpose or direction for the people? Is there a combined national purpose at all? Azadism leaves people to pursue their own interests. It's not ethical to enforce our "Sikh values" on others. People should be free to make their own decisions and suffer the consequences of them, as long as it does not impede the right for others to do the same. This is essentially the only ethic that a Khalsa government needs to enforce. This naturally covers things like: lying, stealing, cheating, murdering, assaulting etc[53].

Sikhs as private citizens can educate and promote Sikhi but just like all other philosophies in an Azadist state, they cannot legally use force to do so. It is only the veracity of their argument that should be considered, and this has to compete in the *free market of ideas*. A similar environment allowed for Sikhi to arise in the first place, and if we are confident in our Guru's teachings, what is there to worry about? The Gurus themselves were comfortable doing this. Guru Tegh Bahadur was touring India doing Parchar at the time of his sons birth (Guru Gobind Singh). And even more recently, take the example of Basics of Sikhi. Bhai Jugraj Singh used to say:

"Sikhi doesn't need selling, it needs telling"

As a result, they have introduced countless into Sikhi through their efforts, including the author of this manifesto[54]. If we as Sikhs want people to live in a certain way we should first live that way ourselves. Kavi Santokh Singh mentions 3 ways in which people can persuade each other[55]:

1.   Through physical force (this is the worst way)

     Historically we can look at Islamic conquests, Christian crusades or other acts by groups throughout history to enforce their ideals on others through force. However, this is an obvious violation of the NAP.

2. Through speech (better)

   Bad ideas should be fought with good ideas. The government's role here is to maintain an environment that allows for free speech and should never introduce state censorship in any form. Alongside this, no media outlet or ideology should be promoted by the state.

3. Through example (this is the best)

   Under this method, any change someone would like to make in their society starts with themselves. This forces people to be critical of their own suggestions as well as maintain people's individual rights to be free to choose how to live their own lives. Since people are generally acting out of their own self-interest, seeing a certain lifestyle choice as providing greater results than their own should persuade them to change. There should also be a level of acceptance that no one lifestyle fits all. People may take what is best for them and leave what doesn't work. Having the freedom to do so is of the utmost importance.

For those lifestyle choices that harm a non-consenting third party, the Khalsa's role is to use force to protect that third party. Those who break this human right for others, they themselves forfeit their own rights to freedom. This alongside mutual contracts are the only exceptions to NAP being legal to be broken.

Contracts and Law

Although the topic of this manifesto centres around economics, as with previous sections on the style of governance, the legal system will again only be briefly touched upon using the same principles on which the economic spheres of an Azadist society stands upon. A future publication may expand upon this either as a follow up to this manifesto or through the Seva of someone else if they so desire.

If substantiated by the courts, two or more consenting parties are free to form a contract giving up their state-protected rights. But this must be backed up by the courts as a third party witness and to determine whether all parties are signing the contract voluntarily and not under duress.

For example, there are many laws and crimes within Islamic law (known as the Sharia), that are not normally legal or illegal in other judicial systems. Therefore, it may be difficult in non-Muslim nations to completely live according to this as it could potentially conflict with existing laws[56]. Since an Azadist society does not punish "victimless crimes", many laws that may be considered punishable within the Sharia may not be punishable on the state level. What Azadism provides is a system in which Muslims are free to impose their laws, but only on Muslims. By formalising a contract, each Muslim that chooses to adhere to these extra sets of laws may register their conviction to do so. If they break a law in the Sharia, then part of that contract would state that they are liable for the appropriate punishment accordingly. A crime that does not break the NAP but is deemed punishable under Sharia can then be dealt with by dedicated Sharia courts. The only way for a Muslim to get out of this is to leave their faith, which will void their contract and place them under the protection of the Khalsa (unless the law broken under Sharia also broke the NAP). Any law system that exists based on religion or any other affiliation, exists in addition to the wider NAP based legal framework upheld by an Azadist government. As long as there is freedom to join and leave these groups, any contract can be drawn up and agreed upon in this manner.

These sorts of contracts are already in existence. Two cage fighters both break the NAP when they fight, but do so with mutual consent. Since both have voluntarily chosen to engage in this competition with each other, there is no problem here that the state needs to step in for. Another example that was more prevalent in the past is duels. Both parties are more than free to write up a contract in which they relieve their opponent of any legal repercussions when one kills or harms the other. But again, it must be stressed that a contract must be written and overseen by a third party witness to ensure that it is indeed mutual. In the beginning, an Azadist court must take on the role to facilitate this and act as that witness.

Azadism does not recognise Sikhi as a religion per se, but the Khalsa order can fit into this category[57]. Khalsa is one particular "way" of expressing Sikhi. Other traditional ways include the Udasis, Nirmale and Sevapanthis, and more recently perhaps the Namdhari Panth or Taksali denominations. However, Sikhi on its own can be followed by anyone, even as Muslims, Hindus or any other religion (or none at all!). Guidance can be taken from the Sri Guru Granth Sahib and the Guru Khalsa Panth to whatever degree, regardless of any other label. For this reason, it makes little sense for "Sikhi" courts to emerge similar to how the Sharia ones could as above. Rather, independent Panthic courts could be established based on individual Rehit Marayade where each "way" of Sikhi can establish their own. Sikhs can then decide to join a specific path, or even none at all. This system is especially the case for the Khalsa structured in a Misl system. Each Misl can set their own Maryada relevant to their own context. If someone wanted to avoid punishment or responsibility they are free to leave and denounce their status. This all takes inspiration again through the Sakhi of the 40 Mukte. The Guru themselves had allowed for apostasy amongst members of the Khalsa through a written contract of sorts, by making them sign a letter of dismissal (which was later ripped up upon request as they returned and attained martyrdom on the battlefield).

The freedom of choice should not be infringed upon unless the NAP is broken. NAP is the foundation on which an Azadist law system is built upon. Those who break the NAP, and harm others without mutual consent, must be held at trial to determine guilt and then subsequently punished in whatever way deemed appropriate by the courts. Any other victimless crime is then dealt with by independent justice systems that sit on top of this and are completely voluntary to participate in - as determined by contracts. Since these "crimes" are victimless, there is less onus on the Azadist courts to step in. So, if someone breaks private law that is not breaking a state law, they either take punishment privately, as permitted by the terms of their contract, or similarly apostatise and relinquish any benefits the contract provided. Consider the case for cannabis. This doesn't affect anyone but the user. If a Nihang Singh wants to make Shaheedi Degh, then he should be free to grow as much marijuana as he wants. He should also be free to carry any weapon he wants, wear whatever Bana he likes and Jhatka whatever animal he owns. Who is the state to tell him no? The only reason a state would need to step in is if the Singh is a bit too Mast and starts throwing the Nughda at people or private property[58].

Again, it must be stressed that not all regions, groups or organisations have to set up private law systems. Sikhs in general do not have to do this for example. The only part which may make sense to have a contract is when a specific order is joined. For Sikhs joining the Khalsa, this may be applied when taking Khande di Pahul. Paper based certificates are already given at Hazur Sahib stating your new name and date, so this could easily be modified to make it contractually binding, where the Hukams given by the Jathedar is clearly expressed in writing.

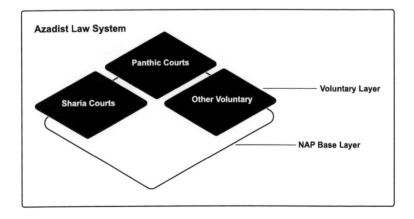

Conclusion

To conclude this manifesto, the following is a brief summary of the key points addressed:

Self-interest is a driving force for the vast majority of human behaviour. Incentives should never be underestimated in their importance in influencing the choices people make. By getting the government out of markets, the propensity for the state to create perverse incentives is drastically reduced. Respecting peoples personal freedoms, and the right for them to transact with each other freely and voluntarily ensures the self-regulation of markets. This way no central planner is needed, as the market itself adapts to shortages and surpluses via the price mechanism and laws of supply and demand. The only time in which a state may need to step in is to either ensure the protection of the market, or prevent those breaking the NAP. Further to this, innovation best arises when private entities are free and unhindered to compete in a NAP based environment. Not only does this advance human potential, but also protects the consumer from monopoly exploitation. Monopolies only exist with the aid of government through lobbying or other means of corporate welfare. Nationalisation of industries is just another form of monopolisation in which the state takes direct control of the production of goods and services. This inevitability leads to uncompetitive entities that are funded by tax-payer money, not voluntary transaction. Therefore, the price mechanism fails, and inefficiencies arise as well as a collapse in innovation. Taxes are inherently unjust, as it is state-mandated theft. Taxes under Azadism would be reformed initially, before being removed entirely in the long-term. Meanwhile, an NIT (or UBI), should be implemented to provide the safety net instead of a welfare state that perpetuates poverty and takes away opportunity. Minimum wages too should be replaced by an NIT, thereby putting pressure off small businesses and onto the state to provide living wages. Private charity replaces much of the social security function that the state formally would have provided. The state now is reduced to these 4 functions initially to be classed as Azadist:

1. National Defence
2. Policing
3. Justice System and Courts
4. Tax administration

From this, the state should gradually reduce its role, and further limit itself out of existence in the long term. Combined with a well-armed populace, a Khalsa government is an ideal candidate to administer this process of handing power back into the hands of the people and away from tyrants. They could be organised as a decentralised Misl system made up of many competing groups, each with their own specialisations and Rehit Maryade. Finally, contracts are a crucial element in allowing different groups to set their own laws on top of the NAP based law system layer.

The level of discourse regarding these issues needs to update. As a Panth, we are so behind in these things it is disappointing. Looking through our history, it is understandable as to why, but nonetheless, this doesn't excuse our present day ignorance. The blood of our Shaheeds is a currency. It has bought us today time and space in which to manoeuvre. We can either waste this resource and stick to old methods of fighting, simply tackling problems head-on without any planning, or become more strategic. Instead of being so reactive, we have to become proactive. Stop waiting around for a problem to arise before acting, for any actions by that point is already too late. It becomes damage control rather than implementing a real solution. This attitude in which we approach problems in the Panth needs to stop. We have become slaves to our emotions and thrown reason out the window. To use logic and reason in matters of Raajniti is to do Khandan of issues, breaking them down into parts and using our Bibek Buddhi to analyse.

ਨਮੋ ਸ੍ਰੀ ਭਗੌਤੀ ਬਢੇਲੀ ਸਰੋਹੀ ॥ ਕਰੇ ਏਕ ਤੇ ਦੈ ਸੁਭਟ ਹਾਥ ਸੋਹੀ ॥

Salutations to the highest Sword, the cutting Sirohi [type of Sword]. Making two from one [decapitating], the warrior who holds You in their hand is victorious !

— Sri Guru Gobind Singh, Bhagauti Astotar

163

But as of now, our faculty to do Khandan is impaired by emotion and leading us to ignorance and bad ideas. We approach situations too readily with our hearts and forget our brains. There is an important place for that in Bhagti, however, we cannot use that same thinking for everything. There is a Sama for each state of mind. This is why on the verge of battle, Guru Gobind Singh would send his court philosophers away on the reasoning that they will spend too much time deliberating and causing doubt. Unhelpful traits for a time like that, but great in times of peace. Understanding how to do Khandan is in itself a form of Shastarvidya, not of physical weapons but of mental. The world has moved on from fighting on horseback and stabbing or shooting our problems won't solve them. Now is a time of information warfare, where ideas are the armies and the mind is the battlefield. There is currently a pandemic of ignorance infecting the Panth. For this reason, we act like sheep when problems arise and are dragged by the ear by perverse agendas and bad ideas. What we as a Panth need is a long-term, well thought out approach that takes into account the lessons of the past. We need to make our principles strong but our techniques fluid. Only then can we avoid future bloodshed and oppression by forces far smarter and resourceful than ourselves. In order to outmanoeuvre the enemy, we have to understand the enemy. But the first steps towards any of this is conquering your own minds. Change begins with yourself. Stop begging at the doorsteps of our enemies and take action in your own hands. Why would a thief grant justice to his victims? Especially when the thief is still plundering the homes of others, why expect compassion from them? Learn to use a system rather than it using you. This manifesto is only one step in this effort. You as the reader are encouraged to further solidify and apply this knowledge.

Whilst debate on the topic of central planning vs free markets is definitely a valid one, the need for advancing the discussion to answer some of the details in this manifesto is perhaps even more important. This is the level of discussion the Panth needs to be at in order to get ahead. If we want to seriously consider the possibility of our own nation state, or reforming an existing one, then sound economics need to be understood and implemented. We do not want to fall into the same pattern as all others before us. For these reasons, the following list of questions are just some areas that require further Vichaar:

- How long should each phase last on the path to full privatisation?
- What should be done about tariffs?
- What is the policy on immigration?
- Is UBI better than NIT?
- What should the threshold income be for a NIT?
- What should the flat tax rate be to begin with?
- What type of tax should be implemented?
- When should taxes be phased out entirely, if at all?
- When does the right to be protected under the NAP apply?
- How would the legal system contain the correct incentives to supply justice and avoid corruption?
- What methods should be implemented to allow for communication between Misls?
- What constitutes as a contract? What are the necessary components of one that clearly define the agreement and avoids future issues? Should a defined template be used?
- What are the rules of engagement in potential battles between Misls?
- How to integrate the latest advancements in technology into systems to reduce bureaucracy?
- Should there be a death penalty?
- What is the stance on patent and intellectual property rights?

These questions will at least be explored further by myself on the accompanying website and social media page. On these platforms, extra resources will be made available and any future publications or posts will be presented here. You as the reader are also encouraged to participate especially.

www.azadism.co.uk

Please get in touch if you would like to help contribute or write economic related articles yourself. The website will also detail some additional resources if you would like to continue learning about economics starting with Milton Friedman's 'Free to Choose' series. Additionally, you are encouraged to look through the resources provided in the Notes sections. Please also follow on social media to keep up to date with future posts and information.

A final note for the Khalsa. Stop looking for leaders to guide you, we already have them as Sikhs. They are our Gurus, and they have given us a wealth of lessons. Abandon a mindset that if we could only get the right person in charge, then things would be so much better. Not only is it almost impossible to find them, but even those who appear strong-willed, moral and of high character can submit to change. This is one of the key lessons in Rattan Singh Bhangu's Panth Prakash in telling the story of Banda Singh Bahadur. Even that person who was given Khande di Pahaul by Guru Gobind Singh themselves were still susceptible to failure. Understand that the Guru decentralised power and gave sovereignty onto the Khalsa Panth as a whole for a reason. Stop acting like beggars and become kings of your own kingdoms. Realise that wherever you put your foot is Khalsa Raj. Develop a love for freedom and oppose all that threaten it. The great philosopher Alan Watts once gave a lecture about happiness. He talked about the difference between how happiness is thought about in the west versus the east. In the west, happiness is something you "attain", an addition to yourself. However, in the east, it is seen as something inherent, that you get to by removing external barriers to it. Freedom is the same. It cannot be given, it is the natural state of all things. Similarly, so is love, compassion, honesty, contentment and humility. These are what is left when the Panj Chor are removed. Even more fundamentally, when the ego itself is removed all you are left with is everything else - God itself. Stop waiting for reincarnations of great Singhs in our past, and instead become great Singhs of today. This is true sovereignty, recognising that the Akaal Purakh outside you is the same one that is inside you. You are that which you seek, if only you take the initiative to recognise what you have been blessed with. Take Raaj, don't be given it.

Notes &
Resources.

This supporting section contains notes, references, and any extra resources or comments that did not fit in the main body of this manifesto. However, this has strayed away from the usual academic conventions regarding bibliographies or reference lists. Instead the emphasis is on disseminating information in the clearest possible way, not just conforming to standard essay writing practices for the sake of it. Therefore, much of this section will not only include references as per a traditional style, but also links and notes on the points made through out the paper. Some of these will be in the form of academic papers and studies, whereas others would be in video formats, including lectures and interviews. The point here is to make it easier for you to immerse yourself in this material by providing the best possible way in which information related to the topics discussed in this manifesto can be portrayed. The author recognises that most people are unlikely to read through the lengthy papers, but may be more open to videos or podcasts for example. Especially discussions and debates. As well as this, certain tangents or topics that did not fit in the main sections would be elaborated upon here. For these reasons this Notes and Resources section is as valuable as the rest of this manifesto and the reader is encouraged to refer to this alongside the main body using the superscripted numbering system throughout the text.

Disclaimer: It should be obvious, however Azadism does not agree with all the views of everyone mentioned in the references. Some of the resources are provided to give extra context, and where there is disagreement about the content itself this will be highlighted. However, it is unreasonable to suggest merely because a certain name was mentioned now that Azadism accepts completely all of the other views outside of that particular reference. It may also be a good idea to archive these resources. All the direct links are available on the website:

www.azadism.co.uk

Introduction

1	Link: <u>Levels of Understanding - by Bhai Mani Singh Shahid (manglacharan.com)</u> Raw: https://www.manglacharan.com/post/levels-of-understanding-by-bhai-mani-singh-shahid I have purposefully decided not to use the term 'Khand' that is mentioned in the translators notes for this since I've found that this is often confused with the Khands used in Japu Ji Sahib when discussing this topic in person. The actual word used in the original text is "Adhkaar" which they translate as competency, which I felt was more appropriate for this instance.
2	Bhai Satpal Singh from Nanak Naam expands upon the deep metaphors present in the Ramayan to extract these key spiritual concepts, available here: Link: <u>Diwali: True Meaning Of Ramayana | Bandi Chorr Divas | Do Sikhs Celebrate Diwali? - YouTube</u> Raw: https://www.youtube.com/watch?v=xX4fKsh6AlY The rest of his YouTube channel is a great resource in English for discovering more than just the basics, with lecture series on Japu Ji Sahib, Anand Sahib and other topics. The approach here is distinctly non-dual and much emphasis is placed on interpreting Bani and Ithiaas through the lens of Ik Onkaar first.
3	Link: <u>Three Chapters of Spiritual Progression - Gobind Gita (manglacharan.com)</u> Raw: https://www.manglacharan.com/post/three-chapters-of-spiritual-progression-gobind-gita I have retranslated some parts of this from Manglacharan's article linked. Antar = within/inside I felt was more accurate than simply "one's mind", although I would agree it achieves a similar purpose of the translation. A few of the English translations throughout have been mended for mistakes and to

make them more accurate. Please take time to read both the original and translations, and let me know if you feel like there have been any errors on my behalf also.

4. In a banned TED talk given by the Biologist Dr Rupert Sheldrake named 'The Science Delusion', he goes through some of the dogmas held within parts of the scientific community that are largely baseless assumptions. One of these was the belief that consciousness was "produced" by the brain, to which Sheldrake suggests that these two may have a different relationship. Instead, he gives the example of a TV signal and the receiver within the TV. The same way the TV signal is always present but only manifests when there is a receiver to capture it to display its contents, similarly, consciousness may also behave similarly. Our brains, therefore, act as the receiver of consciousness rather than the producer.

Link: Rupert Sheldrake - The Science Delusion BANNED TED TALK - YouTube
Raw: https://www.youtube.com/watch?v=JKHUaNAxsTg

The field of Panpsychism is at the forefront of these types of studies, with much of its premise based upon the idea that all things are contained within a sort of mind space, and that the most fundamental building blocks of reality is consciousness itself. This channel is a great introduction to these topics, as well as the accompanying 'Waking Cosmos' podcast, where you can hear interviews with some of the field's top scientists and philosophers.

Link: metaRising - YouTube
Raw: https://www.youtube.com/user/metaRising

5. Bhagat Dhunna similarly was given, to what would most of us today would see, a ritual to observe in the form of worshipping a rock. However, his innocent nature and pure love for God, spilt this "ritual" over to devotion as he refused to eat till the rock (which he thought was God) ate first! If there was no love in this, then he would have been mindlessly worshipping this stone since that was all he was told to do, hence he would have

remained in the state of duality and on the competency of Karma. As the Sakhi goes, the rock does indeed eat the food after God appreciates the level of devotion here, and then Bhagat Dhunna is enlightened. Whereas it can be easily interpreted that his love bore fruit and this is a metaphor to show the listener that this is the power of loving devotion, the fact that he was also enlightened in the story shows he reached the final stage of understanding, Gyaan. How would we react to someone doing this today? We would likely accuse them of idol worship and throw all sorts of Panktis at them to prove they are wrong. However, it is important to recognise that the path of spirituality is indeed a path. Everyone is progressing at their own pace and each are on their own levels. That relationship between the Guru and the Sikh is personal to them alone. Obviously, there are limits to this, but it is still something to think about when observing even the worst people in the world.

6	There is also Pratibhasika - *apparent reality*. In fact, Advaita has many breakdowns and terminology defined for these things, but they have been left out for now for brevity. These two parts are sufficient enough to express the point, however if interested, consult this: Link: Rope-Snake Analogy Using Logic: How Falsehood Becomes Truth (yesvedanta.com) Raw: https://www.yesvedanta.com/rope-snake-logical-analysis-advaita-vedanta-analogy/
7	There are other breakdowns such as in terms of Brahma, Vishnu, and Mahesh (Shiva), but this is my favourite and is often overlooked.
8	Credit must be given here to Harwinder Singh Mander (Naujawani) from where I first heard about this idea that we as a Panth are reactive and not proactive. This one statement is paradigm-shifting in understanding why our community behaves the way it does.

	Link: | naujawani Raw: https://naujawani.com/
9	A separate post will be made on this as a case study since misinformation and misunderstanding of the issue seems to be occurring on both sides.
10	Link: Thomas Sowell Brings the World into Focus through an Economics Lens - YouTube Raw: https://www.youtube.com/watch?v=cdBn7MUM3Yo "... because I want people to read it!"
11	Link: Praxeology: The Methodology of Austrian Economics | Mises Institute Raw: https://mises.org/library/praxeology-methodology-austrian-economics

Section I
Self-Interest

1	It should be made clear here, how I am using the term "spiritual" throughout this manifesto. A "spiritual" effort is understood to mean any effort that makes one closer to achieving oneness/God.
2	Often, a Shabad is more completely understood through experiencing it in the way it was intended - musically. Especially with Raag, this helps reveal the emotions and feelings the Guru is aiming to represent through their words: Link: Kabeer Tu Tu Karta Tu Hooaa - by Dhrupadhamar - BoS 5 Year Anniversary - YouTube Raw: https://www.youtube.com/watch?v=FmxD1QP83II Bhai Kirit Singh and Bhai Jadeep Singh expand on the history of this particular style of singing on their website available here: Link: dhrupadhamar – Dhrupad | Dhamar | Shabad Kirtan Raw: http://www.dhrupadhamar.com/ Another rendition of this Shabad presented here by the Naamdhari Panth, who have done a great Seva in keeping Raag Kirtan traditions alive to sing our Guru's Bani: Link: Kabir Tu Tu Karta Tu Hua | Shabad Kirtan | Raag Des | Jhap Taal | Sri Bhaini Sahib - YouTube Raw: https://www.youtube.com/watch?v=gMqRAW6SnsI
3	This isn't to say that this is the only way the Guru teaches the Sikhs, refer to the translation of Bhai Mani Singh's 'Sikhan di bhagat mala' for the 3 levels of competency and how the Guru caters for all by designing Shabads relevant to each level (See introduction).

4	From Sri Guru Tegh Bahadur's Salok Mahalla 9

Link: 4K - Jo Sukh Ko Chaahai Sada - Bhai Manbir Singh (Australia) - Sri Nankana Sahib - YouTube
Raw: https://www.youtube.com/watch?v=jnex_8N_SVs |
| 5 | Manglacharan.com has been an invaluable resource in uncovering some of the more overlooked aspects of Gurbani and Ithiaas. As well as Gobind Gita and Sikhan Di Bhagat Mala referenced in the introduction, Bhagauti Astotar is another prime example of this as explained in the heading to the translation provided below:

Link: Bhagauti Astotar Translation (manglacharan.com)
Raw: https://www.manglacharan.com/post/bhagauti-astotar-translation |
| 6 | In order to avoid this Manifesto turning into a Gutka, I have decided not to include more Shabads for this point in the body text. However, here are some of the examples mentioned from SikhiToTheMax.org:

Link: Shabad - SikhiToTheMax
Raw: https://www.sikhitothemax.org/shabad?id=1648&q=you%20are%20was&type=3&source=G&highlight=20025

Link: Shabad - SikhiToTheMax
Raw: https://www.sikhitothemax.org/shabad?id=3972&q=by%20the%20hai&type=3&source=G&highlight=47308 |
| 7 | Professor Lou Fenech is a prominent modern day scholar on the study of Sikh history including the Zafarnama and Maharaj's Darbars. The following is an interview conducted by the UK Punjab Heritage Association, where Lou reveals the nature of the |

Guru's courts in more detail:

Link: <u>Prof Lou Fenech on The Court of the Tenth Guru -</u>
<u>YouTube</u>
Raw: https://www.youtube.com/watch?v=CsaXpAmDm10

As well as this, he has devoted a book on this topic, "The Darbar of the Sikh Gurus: The Court of God in the World of Men"

Another notable modern-day scholar in these matters is Satnam Singh from Denmark, whose research has been extremely valuable in opening the doors to what our Guru's Darbars were like in terms of what was studied and the arts and poetry that flourished during that time.

Link: <u>Ratnam Singh ستنام(@satnam sdk) • Instagram photos</u>
<u>and videos</u>
Raw: https://www.instagram.com/satnam_sdk/

8	Link: <u>Levels of Understanding - by Bhai Mani Singh Shahid</u> <u>(manglacharan.com)</u> Raw: https://www.manglacharan.com/post/levels-of-understanding-by-bhai-mani-singh-shahid The above Sakhi from Sikhan Di Bhagat Mala is perhaps one of the most crucial pieces of information we have in understanding how the Guru designed Bani.
9	In economics, these third party effects are known as "Externalities". You can get both positive and negative externalities. The one in this example is a negative, however, cases of positive externalities include beekeepers benefiting from a nearby orchid and vice versa. These don't tend to be an issue for the most part.
10	Link: <u>Systems Thinking and the Cobra Effect - Our World</u> <u>(unu.edu)</u> Raw: https://ourworld.unu.edu/en/systems-thinking-and-the-cobra-effect

Section II
Markets

1	This concept became known as the "division of labour" of which Adam Smith detailed in his work. The following link is an interactive demonstration of one of the analogies given in Smith's Wealth Of Nations about a pin factory: Link: Adam Smith's Enlightened World (adamsmithworks.org) Raw: https://www.adamsmithworks.org/pin_factory.html
2	Unfortunately now, a gold standard is no longer used. President Nixon took the world off of this gold standard in 1971, and onto a dollar-based one backed by nothing but trust in the US government. Link:A Brief History of the Gold Standard, with a Focus on the United States | Mises Wire Raw:https://mises.org/wire/brief-history-gold-standard-focus-united-states Link: WTF Happened In 1971? Raw:https://wtfhappenedin1971.com/ Link: Mises on the gold standard as the symbol of international peace and prosperity (1949) | Online Library of Liberty (libertyfund.org) Raw:https://oll.libertyfund.org/quote/mises-on-the-gold-standard-as-the-symbol-of-international-peace-and-prosperity-1949 Whilst a gold standard was important to help prevent inflationary money printing by governments (and is perhaps much better than what we have now), it still was set by the state as legal tender. Azadism would do away with any state-backed or mandated currency (including gold) and let the people themselves establish their own money through market interactions. If people want to pay in gold that's great, as well any other kind of money such as cryptocurrencies. By separating

money and government, the power of manipulating the money supply is removed. A future publication may expand in more detail the monetary environment of an Azadist state; for this manifesto, it will become too technical. However, it must be stated that alongside the removal of legal-tender laws, Azadism is strictly opposed to any form of central banking. No central bank should have power over the money supply, setting unified interest rates for the nation or acting as a state-backed lender of last resort in an Azadist system.

3   Link: Chapter VI | Adam Smith Works
     Raw: https://www.adamsmithworks.org/documents/chapter-vi-of-the-component-parts-of-the-price-of-commodities

4   Another example may be non-profits, however, even here, owners and workers are still usually paid a salary. Profit is still generated, but it is reinvested into the organisation or goes to the cause that they were set up for instead.

5   This was known as the 'Labour Theory of Value' and was held by many classical economists, including David Ricardo and Karl Marx. This has now been largely debunked and replaced by the Subjective Theory of Value and the Marginal Utility Theory.

     LINK: Three Arguments Debunking Marx's Labor Theory of Value | Mises Wire
     RAW: https://mises.org/wire/three-arguments-debunking-marxs-labor-theory-value

6   Carl Menger was the founder of the Austrian School of Economics. After recognising discrepancies between the ideas of classical economists and his experience with the real world, it led him to critically re-evaluate the entire field of economics. In 1871 he released his work 'Grundsätze der Volkswirtschaftslehre' - Principles of Economics. This diamond example was from the third chapter, accessed here:

	Link: <u>Menger's Principles of Economics: Burying the Labor Theory of Value	Libertarianism.org</u> Raw: https://www.libertarianism.org/essays/mengers-principles-economics-burying-labor-theory-value
7	This is a common example used to explain the Subjective Theory of Value. Each person values goods differently depending on their own personal preferences.
8	This is covered by the Marginal Utility Theory, which states that after a point, each additional unit of a good that is consumed would provide gradually less satisfaction or utility than the previous unit. Link: <u>Marginal utility	economics	Britannica</u> Raw: <u>https://www.britannica.com/topic/marginal-utility</u>
9	Link: <u>The Value of Diamonds and Water Paradox (investopedia.com)</u> Raw: https://www.investopedia.com/ask/answers/032615/how-can-marginal-utility-explain-diamondwater-paradox.asp Link: <u>Value and Prices - (Austrian Econ Basics #2) - YouTube</u> Raw: https://www.youtube.com/watch?v=4vmSBppSGzY
10	Examples of these are markets for *human beings,* such as slavery and human trafficking. Since these both violate the NAP, they are not compatible with the idea of *Free* Markets as interpreted by Azadism. The parties involved here have not all consented and so transactions of this nature should be resisted to maintain freedom. Alternatively, markets for drugs do not break the NAP, since both buyer and seller have consented to this transaction. No freedom has been eroded in this case. This may seem immoral initially to allow drug trades to be legal, however, this may be

expanded in a later post to dispel some of the misunderstanding around legalisation and decriminalisation of drugs.

11	Link: Price Controls - Econlib Raw: https://www.econlib.org/library/Enc/PriceControls.html
12	Link: Friedrich Hayek (Stanford Encyclopedia of Philosophy) Raw: https://plato.stanford.edu/entries/friedrich-hayek/ Hayek was perhaps one of the greatest minds in the last century regarding economics. When he moved to London in 1931 he provided strong resistance against the ideas of John Meynard Keynes. However, unfortunately, Keynes succeeded in the public sphere, with many of the modern western so-called "capitalist" economies adopting varying degrees of Keynesian policies as a result. For more information about this debate, see here: Link: The clash between Keynes and Hayek defined modern economics | British Politics and Policy at LSE Raw: https://blogs.lse.ac.uk/politicsandpolicy/keynes-hayek-nicholas-wapshott/
13	Link: History of the OED | Oxford English Dictionary Raw: https://public.oed.com/history/ Link: How the Oxford English Dictionary started out like Wikipedia | WIRED UK Raw: https://www.wired.co.uk/article/the-oxford-english-wiktionary

Other Useful Resources:

Please take some time to understand Supply and Demand, as it is a crucial element of economics.

Link: <u>Law of Supply and Demand Definition (investopedia.com)</u>
Raw: https://www.investopedia.com/terms/l/law-of-supply-demand.asp

Link: <u>Explaining supply and demand - Economics Help</u>
Raw: https://www.economicshelp.org/blog/160660/economics/explaining-supply-and-demand-2/

Link: <u>Simulating Supply and Demand - YouTube</u>
Raw:https://www.youtube.com/watch?v=PNtKXWNKGN8&list=PLxUfDdw5RjEIB4aWVJWYvltl5uey7h-Ej&index=3

Understanding of the pricing mechanism and markets forms the basis of economic thinking. This is only a brief summary of these concepts, and in order to avoid this paper becoming an economics textbook, it is recommended that the curious look into this further for a deeper understanding. I have included only as much as required for the purposes of this manifesto and as an introduction to arguably the most important concepts in economics and human behaviour as a whole. Some of the concepts mentioned in this section included: supply and demand, opportunity costs, subjective theory of value and marginal utility theory.

Section III
Private vs Public

1	Oxford Dictionary Definition: "business or industry that is managed by independent companies or private individuals rather than being controlled by the state."
2	In fact, even the Oxford dictionary definition leaves room for some ambiguity by introducing the word "direct" in their definition of the 'Private Sector'. Azadism pushes this further and explicitly states that any sort of state control, whether direct or indirect, thereby invalidates any organisation's status as a "private" entity. This better matches with the definition included in the Oxford Dictionary Of Economics and common use of this term I have come across listening to Economists.
3	A note on the incident regarding the Masands being turned into pakore. This was justified on the Guru's behalf since the Masands were not only refusing to comply with the Guru's orders to readdress the donations made by the Sangat (meant for the Guru, the Masands just collected on his behalf) to the Khalsa, but also burnt a Saroop of the Sri Guru Granth Sahib, and conspired to depose him. Thereby, the Guru dealt with them as people who break the NAP and steal the private property of others. A more detailed account is available in Rattan Singh's 'Prachin Panth Prakash' (who in turn refers to Gur Bilas for even more detail).
4	However, I do recognise the role of Hukam in decision making (or lack thereof), however as stated in the introduction, for the purpose of this manifesto I simply have to assume free-will and personal agency for the sake of practicality. At a certain level in this topic specifically, there will be an inability to talk about any of these concepts otherwise.

5	This is a simplistic breakdown in order to highlight the key points. However, sometimes it may be okay that temporarily a particular venture incurs a loss in the short term. This is most often the case with new businesses that may have paid large fixed costs to begin with. However, by examining their cash flow statements or other factors, you can reveal a more accurate reason as to why a business may not be generating profit. However, in the long term, breaking even or making a profit would be needed. Even charities must generate a profit, by ensuring the donations cover their costs.
6	Link: <u>Gurdwara Sri Mal Akhara Sahib	Historical Gurdwara Tours - YouTube</u> Raw: https://www.youtube.com/watch?v=5tXbgyyGZrY
7	Do not look into Robert Greene, nor his book "33 Strategies or War" in particular.
8	Link: <u>The Art of War by Sun Tzu - Chapter 11: The Nine Situations (suntzusaid.com)</u> Raw: https://suntzusaid.com/book/11 This website is good resource for reading this text due to the added commentary
9	Or at the very least more than otherwise. In fact, even this Manifesto would not have been written without employing elements of this strategy to help motivate and remain disciplined in this endeavour.
10	Link: <u>Rasna Raam Raam Bakhaan - by Dhrupadhamar - BoS 5 Year Anniversary - YouTube</u> Raw: https://www.youtube.com/watch?v=I4aCYT6oSDs

11	Link: The Philosophy And Principles of Capitalism with Yaron Brook (thewealthstandard.com)
	Raw: https://thewealthstandard.com/the-philosophy-and-principles-of-capitalism-with-yaron-brook/
12	The original essay is available here:
	Link: I, Pencil by Leonard E. Read - Foundation for Economic Education (fee.org)
	Raw: https://fee.org/resources/i-pencil-audio-pdf-and-html
	Chicago School economist and Nobel Laureate, Milton Friedman, also talks through this example briefly here:
	Link: Milton Friedman - I, Pencil - YouTube
	Raw: https://www.youtube.com/watch?v=67tHtpac5ws
	Relevant point:
	Link: Carl Sagan's apple pie - YouTube
	Raw: https://www.youtube.com/watch?v=BkHCO8f2TWs
13	Failures in pollution control and climate change are important topics that will be discussed in a future publication, but for the curious please look into the concept of the "Tragedy of the Commons". Maintaining property rights are an important component of an Azadist economy but discussion of this goes outside of the scope of this Manifesto.
	The 2008 Financial crisis is another one of these topics that go outside of the scope of this manifesto too. Explaining this example is too detailed for here, and so may either be discussed elsewhere alongside interest rates, inflation, banking, investing and monetary policy as its own publication. The reader is therefore encouraged to research Peter Schiff's explanation of the topic, someone who predicted and warned everyone long before it happened. His book 'Crash Proof' looks at this subject in detail, but you can also refer to his 2007 Google Talk here (In short, this was government's fault too unsurprisingly):

Link: <u>Crash Proof | Peter Schiff | Talks at Google - YouTube</u>
Raw: https://www.youtube.com/watch?v=tU8jCa_dKTM

Also related and worth the watch is his debates at the Occupy Wall Street protests after the 2008 crash, in which he combats some of the common misconceptions around the situation.

Link: <u>Peter Schiff at Occupy Wall Street "I am the 1%. Let's Talk"</u>
Raw: https://www.youtube.com/watch?v=RYoRoNpIdQQ

14	Link: <u>How Government Regulations Make Housing Unaffordable	Mises Wire</u> Raw: https://mises.org/wire/how-government-regulations-make-housing-unaffordable
15	Link: <u>Price Controls - Econlib</u> Raw: https://www.econlib.org/library/Enc/PriceControls.html
16	Link: <u>Rent Control Does Not Make Housing More Affordable	Manhattan Institute (manhattan-institute.org)</u> Raw: https://www.manhattan-institute.org/issues-2020-rent-control-does-not-make-housing-more-affordable
17	This already exists currently too. Builders themselves recommend private inspectors to check the work over the local councils ones (in the UK) since the latter are often so late in responding, which halts the work as they can not progress without a pass from the inspector. Therefore private ones are preferred since it helps keep building projects on schedule.
18	Government-mandated licences are another headache of state intervention. Esteemed economist Walter E Williams has a great example of Taxi licences that was too lengthy to include here, and the housing regulations already acted as the relevant example for this topic. Nonetheless, the reader is highly encouraged to hear Walter's Williams argument on this topic:

	Link: "Good Intentions" with Walter E. Williams - YouTube Raw: https://www.youtube.com/watch?v=L5TS8QUJWX0
19	Link: Private Regulation: A Real Alternative for Regulatory Reform (cato.org) Raw: https://www.cato.org/sites/cato.org/files/pubs/pdf/pa-303.pdf
20	What about people lying? Companies would likely find ways around this to help build confidence and trust with their consumers. Even now, a lot of the applications on the Google Play Store have the developers respond directly to problems openly so that everyone can see, showing they are happy to support or find a solution. Other methods could be similar to what Amazon does by giving a verified purchase tag. And lastly, other customers of that product themselves can refute the baseless claims.
21	One famous example is Sri Guru Tegh Bahadur sacrificing his own life, alongside his companions Bhai Dayal Das, Bhai Mati Das and Bhai Sati Das, to resist the state from enforcing its religion on private individuals (the Kashmiri Pandits in this case). The freedom of religion is paramount in ensuring a free society, and when the state regulates even this most basic of rights, it is nothing but a sign of tyranny.
22	Link: Milton Friedman - Equality and Freedom (Q&A) Debunking Social Justice Theory - YouTube Raw: https://www.youtube.com/watch?v=5_mGlqyW_Zw&list=PLOv-GldVeFiXd1exZUoQLYC6ynwkQwbvz&index=36
23	Link: Mixing Business With Politics: A Meta-Analysis of the Antecedents and Outcomes of Corporate Political Activity Raw: https://master-cca.cnam.fr/html/ms/cca/articles/article4-4.pdf

24	Link: <u>The Failure of Free Entry (nber.org)</u>
	Raw:
	https://www.nber.org/system/files/working_papers/w26001/
	w26001.pdf
25	Although antitrust laws were designed specifically to combat monopolies, its actual effect was to create a system of extortion. These regulations are used as a weapon by government to threaten successful companies to fill the pockets of politicians.
	Link: <u>Anti-Trust Law and Lawlessness, by Dr. Thomas Sowell	Creators Syndicate</u>
	Raw: https://www.creators.com/read/thomas-sowell/04/15/anti-trust-law-and-lawlessness#decreaseFont
	Link: <u>Do Antitrust Laws Preserve Competition?	Mises Institute</u>
	Raw: https://mises.org/library/do-antitrust-laws-preserve-competition
	Link: <u>Policy Forum: "Milton Friedman on business suicide"	Cato Institute</u>
	Raw: https://www.cato.org/policy-report/march/april-1999/policy-forum-milton-friedman-business-suicide
26	Link: <u>How Microsoft learned ABCs of D.C. - POLITICO</u>
	Raw: https://www.politico.com/story/2011/04/how-microsoft-learned-abcs-of-dc-052483
27	Link: <u>Microsoft Corp Lobbyists • OpenSecrets</u>
	Raw: https://www.opensecrets.org/federal-lobbying/clients/lobbyists?cycle=2019&id=D000000115
	Open Secrets is a non-profit devoted to tracking lobbying expenditure in the US.

28	In fact, it's very difficult to become that large in the first place without government assistance. In principle, larger firms inevitably become increasingly inefficient due to their inability to accurately calculate prices internally.
	Link: Is There a Limit to How Big a Corporation Can Get? | Mises Wire
	Raw: https://mises.org/wire/there-limit-how-big-corporation-can-get
	Link: Why the Economy Isn't Controlled by One Big Corporation | Mises Wire
	Raw: https://mises.org/wire/why-economy-isnt-controlled-one-big-corporation
	On "Economies of scale":
	Link: Per Bylund on the Economics of Value versus Economies of Scale | Mises Institute
	Raw: https://mises.org/library/bylund-economics-value-versus-economies-scale
29	Link: Predatory prosecution (forbes.com)
	Raw: https://www.forbes.com/forbes/1999/0503/6309089a.html?sh=6d014480206f
30	For example:
	Link: Operating room inefficiencies costing the NHS 300,000 operations a year (nationalhealthexecutive.com)
	Raw: https://www.nationalhealthexecutive.com/Health-Care-News/operating-room-inefficiencies-costing-the-nhs-300000-operations-a-year

The following shows further the extent of the problem. Whilst Azadism would disagree with the proposed solution of more investment (i.e throw more money at it), it is a useful report nonetheless to show how inefficient public sector industries become due to various restrictions and regulations that lead to shortages such as these.

Link: Medical staffing in the NHS in England report (bma.org.uk)
Raw: https://www.bma.org.uk/advice-and-support/nhs-delivery-and-workforce/workforce/medical-staffing-in-england-report

31	However, staunch defenders of this system would still stress the cultural importance of the NHS, as something that has undeniably been seeped into the hearts and minds of the British public. Azadism sees this as no different from forcibly maintaining the British royal family, similarly through taxes. If people want to voluntarily pay for these "cultural" enterprises, they should pay for it themselves, and all those who don't should be free to opt-out. This forces the NHS to stay competitive as its income is now based on its ability to meet the needs of its "customers", and not on the state stealing peoples money to force them to pay for it. This would also give room for other competitors to come into the space and introduce necessary improvements.
32	Link: How does health spending in the U.S. compare to other countries? - Peterson-KFF Health System Tracker Raw: https://www.healthsystemtracker.org/chart-collection/health-spending-u-s-compare-countries/#item-start
33	Link: Are Patents Impeding Medical Care and Innovation? (nih.gov) Raw: https://www.ncbi.nlm.nih.gov/pmc/articles/PMC2795161/

Whilst the above admits that patents do indeed increase costs and restrict innovation, they do not suggest doing away with this system entirely. Further debate and research on this are needed in which we can compare reforming patents with alternatives such as the prize system mentioned in the article. However, from an Azadist perspective, any state-backed mandates protecting specific organisations over others is inherently wrong and counter-productive.

34   For more information on how the US Healthcare system works, please consult the following (although it is now a bit old):

Link: A layman's guide to the U.S. health care system (nih.gov)
Raw:
https://www.ncbi.nlm.nih.gov/pmc/articles/PMC4193322/

As we can see it is not as private as it is so often claimed to be. Instead, it is a mess of government intervention and funding, combined with highly regulated industries.

35   Link: Human Experimentation: An Introduction to the Ethical Issues (pcrm.org)
Raw: https://www.pcrm.org/ethical-science/human-experimentation-an-introduction-to-the-ethical-issues

Link: What We Know About the CIA's Midcentury Mind-Control Project | Smart News | Smithsonian Magazine
Raw: https://www.smithsonianmag.com/smart-news/what-we-know-about-cias-midcentury-mind-control-project-180962836/

Link: 'Poisoner In Chief' Details The CIA's Secret Quest For Mind Control : NPR
Raw: https://www.npr.org/2019/09/09/758989641/the-cias-secret-quest-for-mind-control-torture-lsd-and-a-poisoner-in-chief?t=1639130317802

36	Singhs who aim to be 'Tyar Bar Tyar' should be so in a multitude of ways. Smart financial planning and insurance should be part of this. Especially the Naujuwan and Bhujangis - health insurance is cheaper if you are young and healthy.
37	This is not to say that all adults are therefore by default acting rationally, but for the most part, they have a far higher probability to do so than a child can due to the time taken to develop mentally being longer. This should be taken as a rule of thumb; there are obviously many exceptions to this for which there would be appropriate support mechanisms in place that will be touched upon in the next section.
38	Adults would not have this right, since the state has no justification to force adults into education if they do not want to, as this would break their rights associated with NAP. Hence why these rights are 'swapped' for children. Technically education isn't a right in the same way that free speech is a right. It is an entitlement, something that you are given, not restricted from. The distinction between positive rights (entitlements) and negative rights (liberties) are important to understand, the following two clips give a better outline of these concepts: Link: Basic Human Rights Explained | Alex Gladstein and Lex Fridman - YouTube Raw: https://www.youtube.com/watch?v=pZKS3eS44tA Link: Positive Rights vs. Negative Rights | Learn Liberty Raw: https://www.learnliberty.org/videos/positive-rights-vs-negative-rights/

39	"Property" is the only word that seemed appropriate in this context. However, unlike all other property, they can't be bought and sold but they do have assigned relationships with people who are responsible for them.
40	Free to Choose is a book based on the 1980s 10 part TV series by the same name and presented by Economist Milton Friedman themselves. The TV series will be linked to at end of these notes as one of the valuable next steps in understanding this subject area. See Page 170 (181 of the PDF), available here: Link: Free To Choose: A Personal Statement (unam.mx) Raw: https://bit.ly/3FqZ7IQ
41	"The education, or rather the uneducation, of black children from low income families is undoubtedly the greatest disaster area in public education and its most devastating failure. This is doubly tragic for it has always been the official ethic of public schooling that it was the poor and the oppressed who were its greatest beneficiaries." Ibid page 151 (162 of the PDF)
42	Link: Why Milton Friedman Saw School Choice as a First Step, Not a Final One - Foundation for Economic Education (fee.org) Raw: https://fee.org/articles/why-milton-friedman-saw-school-choice-as-a-first-step-not-a-final-one/
43	Link: Education System in North Korea - NGO - PSCORE Raw: http://pscore.org/life-north-korea/forced-to-hate/
44	The same reasoning applies to media also. Under Azadism there is no justification for any sort of state-owned or funded (whether wholly or in part) media organisation whatsoever. In

	the UK the BBC would be an example of this.
45	It could be argued that sometimes subjects are studied for enjoyment rather than employment, and this is completely fine. If there is a market for that, then those things will be available. This is actually more in line with what universities were originally meant to be, centres to further knowledge out of curiosity rather than to secure employment necessarily.
46	Link: Relavance of Gurukul System of Education in our Modern Education System to Transform the Engineering Education, An Experimental Study.pdf (ijiet.com) Raw: http://ijiet.com/wp-content/uploads/2016/12/1158.pdf I'm unsure how scientific his experiment was in this paper, and it was quite obvious he was biased. But so is this manifesto, so oh well.
47	The rate at which student loans are paid back as of December 2020 is 25% Link: Student loan statistics - House of Commons Library (parliament.uk) Raw: https://commonslibrary.parliament.uk/research-briefings/sn01079/
48	Link: Peter Schiff: The Government Created the Student Loan Bubble | SchiffGold Raw: https://schiffgold.com/peters-podcast/peter-schiff-the-government-created-the-student-loan-bubble/
49	Again, the laws of supply and demand determine this. Those things that are in abundance but the demand does not match or rise with it, naturally reduces their "price" - in this case the worth or value of the degree.

Other Useful Resources:

Link: Regulations Improve the Free Market? - Foundation for Economic Education (fee.org)
Raw: https://fee.org/articles/regulations-improve-the-free-market/

Link: Why Government is the Problem Milton Friedman 1993 (hoover.org)
Raw:
https://www.hoover.org/sites/default/files/uploads/documents/friedman-government-problem-1993.pdf

Link: Why We Need To Re-think Friedman's Ideas About Monopolies (promarket.org)
Raw: https://promarket.org/2021/04/25/milton-friedman-monopoly-self-interest/

Link: Antitrust Policy Is Both Harmful and Useless | Mises Institute
Raw: https://mises.org/library/antitrust-policy-both-harmful-and-useless

Link: Positive and Negative Liberty (Stanford Encyclopedia of Philosophy)
Raw: https://plato.stanford.edu/entries/liberty-positive-negative/

Section IV
Taxes, Welfare and Safety Nets

1	Link: Income inequality measures (nih.gov) Raw: https://www.ncbi.nlm.nih.gov/pmc/articles/PMC2652960/
2	Link: Inequality - Poverty gap - OECD Data Raw: https://data.oecd.org/inequality/poverty-gap.htm Link: GDP and spending - Gross domestic product (GDP) - OECD Data Raw: https://data.oecd.org/gdp/gross-domestic-product-gdp.htm
3	Link: The Likelihood of Experiencing Relative Poverty over the Life Course (plos.org) Raw: https://journals.plos.org/plosone/article?id=10.1371/journal.pone.0133513
4	Link: Relative vs Absolute Poverty: Defining Different Types of Poverty (habitatforhumanity.org.uk) Raw: https://www.habitatforhumanity.org.uk/blog/2018/09/relative-absolute-poverty/
5	Link: Evidence shows significant income mobility in the US – 73% of Americans were in the 'top 20%' for at least a year | American Enterprise Institute - AEI Raw: https://www.aei.org/carpe-diem/evidence-shows-significant-income-mobility-in-the-us-73-of-americans-were-in-the-top-20-for-at-least-a-year/
6	Link: (PDF) The Life Course Dynamics of Affluence (researchgate.net)

Raw:
https://www.researchgate.net/publication/271598246_The_Life
_Course_Dynamics_of_Affluence

| 7 | Link: The Zero-Sum Fallacy \| Povertycure |
| | Raw: https://www.povertycure.org/learn/issues/charity-hurts/zero-sum-fallacy |

8	Link: Gapminder
	Raw: https://www.gapminder.org/
	Definitely take some time to go through some of the "Upgrade your worldview" surveys here. Hans Gosling has some great Ted Talks too available on YouTube or here:
	Link: TED Talks
	Raw: https://www.ted.com/talks?sort=relevance&q=gapminder

9	Link: Optimistic facts and charts that show the world is getting much, much better - Vox
	Raw: https://www.vox.com/2014/11/24/7272929/global-poverty-health-crime-literacy-good-news
	Often it is a good idea to put the common pessimistic narrative that is pushed by media into context. This isn't to ignore present issues or to say that things will not get worse, but it is important to understand that things can exist in both micro and macro cycles. Focusing too much on the short-term and recent events leads to a very bleak view of the world and where we are headed. Sometimes putting things into perspective and taking a look at the big picture is helpful.
	Matt Ridley's book 'Rational Optimist' highlights many of these examples in more detail. You can hear his Google talk here:
	Link: The Rational Optimist | Matt Ridley | Talks at Google - YouTube
	Raw:

	https://www.youtube.com/watch?v=qMxe73iJPbo&list=PLxUfD dw5RjEJc_uuNrkXyNgUHonoTP6L8&index=6 And his interview with psychologist Jordan Peterson here: Link: <u>Rational Optimism	Matt Ridley - Jordan B Peterson Podcast S4 E5 - YouTube</u> Raw: https://www.youtube.com/watch?v=kjqEMqOyUr8
10	Link: <u>Senator Sanders and the Fixed Pie Fallacy	Cato at Liberty Blog</u> Raw: https://www.cato.org/blog/senator-sanders-fixed-pie-fallacy
11	Link: <u>Chaaban Wealth Management Group - The rule of 72 (rbcwealthmanagement.com)</u> Raw: https://ca.rbcwealthmanagement.com/dian.chaaban/blog/1566725-The-rule-of-72 Link: <u>Rule of 72 Definition, Formula, & Calculation (investopedia.com)</u> Raw: https://www.investopedia.com/terms/r/ruleof72.asp
12	In later posts, investing will be explored further. It is crucial that young people especially learn about how to best manage their finances. The earlier you start the better opportunity you will have.
13	Link: <u>Population Control Isn't the Answer to Climate Change. Capitalism Is. - YouTube</u> Raw: https://www.youtube.com/watch?v=4xkXjj6dalM
14	Azadism is not blinded by hatred for an enemy and instead seeks to learn from them. It is only by understanding the enemy, can

you find their weaknesses, and perhaps more importantly your own. How were they successful? How did they fail? Learning from the enemy is crucial in developing a strategy to defeat them. The enemy is one of the greatest Ustaads.

Sri Guru Gobind Singh Maharaj even seems to praise Auranga in his Zafarnamah too. Perhaps the Guru did this to help educate his Khalsa to similarly show respect to an enemy as means of being strategic.

(page 26)
Link: ZAFARNAMAA WITH PERSIAN.pdf (archive.org)
Raw:
https://ia600303.us.archive.org/24/items/ZafarnamaWithMean ings/ZafarnamaWithMeanings.pdf

15	Khushwant Singh's 'A history of the Sikhs' details this and why it never materialised in Chapter 17 - *Dreams of Sindh and the Sea* Who knows what the state of Panjab would have been today if he had succeeded in his ambitions?
16	Link: The Position of the Zamindars in the Mughal Empire - S. Nurul Hasan, 1964 (sagepub.com) Raw: https://journals.sagepub.com/doi/abs/10.1177/00194646640010 0401?journalCode=iera
17	It is likely this restriction of freedom actively stunted the growth of the US and harmed their rate of progress. By actively suppressing a nation's labour and expertise, the rate of innovation would not reach its full potential.
18	Again, it must not be forgotten that these freedoms were catered towards the invaders, not the enslaved or the natives.
19	Patents are essentially property rights over ideas. It is questionable whether these are acceptable under an Azadist

framework since they must be backed by the state and restrict competition and innovation. Further debate is encouraged in this, however.

Patents were originally granted by Kings to grant exclusive rights to certain subjects (essentially a monopoly backed by the monarchy).

20 A later publication will be produced on the topic of banking and interest rates. However for now it is important to add that the competitive banking system in the US (and elsewhere) was ruined through the introduction of central banks and monetary policies that set interest rates via a central planner and not through market forces. Azadism does not advocate for central banking, or any type of monopoly in this sector - especially not a state-backed one. Again, this will be expanded elsewhere outside this manifesto.

21 Link: 2021 Index of Economic Freedom | The Heritage Foundation
Raw: https://www.heritage.org/index/about

22 Link: Jordan Peterson Talks Gun Control, Angry Men and Women CEOs | Time
Raw: https://time.com/5175974/jordan-peterson-12-rules-book-interview/

23 Validity of such thinking could be put under scrutiny, as with many other of his ideas. Especially those ideas presented in the Communist Manifesto which was put together by Karl Marx and Friedrich Engels. A specific critique of some of the ideas he presents is beyond the scope of this particular publication, and so may be expanded upon elsewhere (particularly Marx's 10 measures he outlines in chapter 2). Instead, I encourage you to see Jordan Peterson's critique here:

	Link: Jordan Peterson's Critique of the Communist Manifesto - YouTube Raw: https://www.youtube.com/watch?v=j_MXSE3wUT4
24	However, please see the following for a more comprehensive review of this topic that goes into further details regarding inequality. If we want to solve some of the issues associated with this, then it is imperative we understand the problem accurately and dispel misconceptions. The following lecture is a great breakdown of this topic by Professor Antony Davies with Learn Liberty. Link: Prof. Antony Davies: 5 Myths About Inequality - YouTube Raw: https://www.youtube.com/watch?v=Jtxuy-GJwC0 Profit when obtained in a **free-market** environment is key here.
25	Link: Can You Be Spiritual and Rich At The Same Time? [Podcast Clips] @BoS TV - YouTube Raw: https://www.youtube.com/watch?v=zYtQgITXY4M&list=PLxUfDdw5RjEIB4aWVJWYvltl5uey7h-Ej&index=23
26	Although, Economist Art Laffer has a unique, but perhaps more accurate spin on the Robin Hood myth: (Listen from 12:20 onwards) Link: Why Raising Taxes Destroys The Economy - Art Laffer - YouTube Raw: https://www.youtube.com/watch?v=GChpnX44_Ns&t=298s
27	Link: Moving my business to Ireland (thinkbusiness.ie) Raw: https://www.thinkbusiness.ie/articles/moving-business-to-ireland/

28	Link: Tax_Rates_and_Migration_Davies_Pulito_WP1131.pdf (mercatus.org) Raw: https://www.mercatus.org/system/files/Tax_Rates_and_Migration_Davies_Pulito_WP1131.pdf
29	This is not just theory, as this is already the case in many of the developed nations that are increasingly imposing these policies. From the US many high-income earners have moved to Puerto Rico for example, in order to avoid the extortionately high tax rates. 'Nomad Capitalist' is run by an entrepreneur who helps provide information and advice to (primarily wealthy) individuals looking to escape exploitation at the hands of the government seeking to take their wealth. Their very motto is "Go where you a treated best". Link: Nomad Capitalist | Offshore Tax and Lifestyle Strategies for Entrepreneurs Raw: https://nomadcapitalist.com/ (Also check out their YouTube channel)
30	"Trickle Down" Theory and "Tax Cuts for the Rich" - Thomas Sowell, page 3, available here: Link: Sowell_TrickleDown.indd (hoover.org) Raw: https://www.hoover.org/sites/default/files/uploads/documents/Sowell_TrickleDown_FINAL.pdf
31	Link: Prof. Antony Davies: 10 Myths About Government Debt - YouTube

	Raw: https://www.youtube.com/watch?v=EPjrFjAxwlw&list=PLxUfDdw5RjEIB4aWVJWYvltl5uey7h-Ej&index=20

Myth #5 and #6, further reinforces Sowell's argument specifically. The rest of the lectures that he did with Learn Liberty are invaluable too. |
| 32 | Alternatively, consumption or Land-revenue taxes may be more in line with Azadist principles (at least for the beginning), however this may be explored in later publications or discussions. |
| 33 | Link: Tax History Project -- Milton Friedman Dead at 94
Raw: http://www.taxhistory.org/thp/readings.nsf/ArtWeb/629A48DB6BB63EDD8525730800064E63?OpenDocument |
| 34 | Link: Free Rider Problem Definition (investopedia.com)
Raw: https://www.investopedia.com/terms/f/free_rider_problem.asp

Link: Free Rider HD - Draw tracks and race bikes
Raw: https://www.freeriderhd.com/ |
| 35 | 'The World Says No to War: Demonstrations against the War on Iraq' by Stefaan Walgrave and Dieter Rucht, available here:

Link: 00 Front_Walgrave (uantwerpen.be)
Raw: https://medialibrary.uantwerpen.be/oldcontent/container2608/files/Walgrave%20Rucht%20(2010)%20-%20The%20world%20says%20no%20to%20war.pdf |
| 36 | Admittedly, direct taxes are not the only way those things can be funded, as the government can take on debt and use disastrous policies to "print more money", which is then acts as an indirect |

tax through inflation. However, this is beyond the scope of this particular publication and may be discussed in greater detail elsewhere. In the meantime, Azadism rejects central banks and even legal tender laws. These must be abolished and never allowed to arise in order to establish and maintain an Azadist state.

37   This manifesto will not detail the pros and cons of each. A future post may go into this further, or a member of the Sangat can take on this Seva. Regardless, debate is encouraged specifically in these areas especially. The conclusion will state more questions and topic areas for further discussion also.

38   Although, under the definitions that Azadism is working with, this would not be classed as a tax anyway.

39   Even other traditions like Christianity saw them as morally deficient and in need of spiritual support:

Link: Why does the Bible speak so negatively about tax collectors? | GotQuestions.org
Raw: https://www.gotquestions.org/Bible-tax-collectors.html

40   Link: "Collect your tax...on the edge of my Kharag" Guru Gobind Singh Ji - Suraj Prakash (manglacharan.com)
Raw: https://www.manglacharan.com/post/collect-your-tax-on-the-edge-of-my-kharag-guru-gobind-singh-ji-suraj-prakash

Again, it must be stressed that although the Guru is indeed representing the supreme ideal of Azadism here, it is not strategic as of right now to replicate the Guru exactly the same way today (although the author would give great respect to those that do take a strong stance like this now). Instead we need to recognise the principle here, that if the Khalsa claims to be sovereign, why then should it promote taxes? Instead, work towards reducing this and removing support from all those who

	aim to increase this state-sanctioned theft. The first step in doing so is at the very least recognising that taxes is something we want to reduce not increase.
41	Although heavily popularised by Milton Friedman, the idea did precede him as it was first attributed to the British writer and Liberal Party politician Juliet Rhys-Williams in the early 1940s.
42	Link: Work-life balance: Why we should only work 15 hours a week (smh.com.au) Raw: https://www.smh.com.au/business/workplace/worklife-balance-why-we-should-only-work-15-hours-a-week-20170817-gxyfk2.html
43	Link: Universal basic income seems to improve employment and well-being | New Scientist Raw: https://www.newscientist.com/article/2242937-universal-basic-income-seems-to-improve-employment-and-well-being/
44	As of writing this manifesto, the author is currently leaning towards NIT being the better system for these initial stages. Although, given a compelling enough argument or observing results of new experiments, this opinion may change. Alternatively, a new method entirely could be proposed to provide a basic income, which is also absolutely fine. This philosophy will adapt towards the best, most up-to-date reasoning of the time given that the principles of Azadism are maintained. This approach is inspired by the Guru's themselves with how they applied Sikhi. The actual principles must remain solid, but the techniques can be fluid. One example of this is the principle of remaining Shastardhari, where the technique to do this is not restricted to just a knife or sword, but axes, spears and guns too. Even a 4 man surface-to-air missile system is acceptable. This

	dichotomy is also seen in the different Sampardaye. Each one of them is just a different technique of expressing Sikhi.
45	Link: <u>Milton Friedman on Healthcare and the Poor - YouTube</u> Raw: https://www.youtube.com/watch?v=iHv4eUJfodA
46	Link: <u>Myth or Measurement: What Does the New Minimum Wage Research Say about Minimum Wages and Job Loss in the United States? | NBER</u> Raw: https://www.nber.org/papers/w28388?utm_campaign=ntwh& utm_medium=email&utm_source=ntwg2 "Our key conclusions are: (i) there is a clear preponderance of negative estimates in the literature; (ii) this evidence is stronger for teens and young adults as well as the less-educated; (iii) the evidence from studies of directly-affected workers points even more strongly to negative employment effects; and (iv) the evidence from studies of low-wage industries is less one-sided."
47	Link: <u>Private Charity versus Government Entitlements (manufacturedhomepronews.com)</u> Raw: https://www.manufacturedhomepronews.com/wp-content/uploads/2018/08/PrivateCharityVersusGovernmentEntitlementsSoftwareMetricsDailyBusinessNewsMHProNews.pdf
48	As the old saying goes: "Give a man a fish and he will eat for a day, teach a man how to fish and you feed him for a lifetime" Unfortunately the wisdom of the statement has been lost amongst those promoting equal outcomes over equal opportunity. They understanding this no more clearer than Bantu Holomisa had said it... Link: <u>Bantu Holomisa - you give a poor man a fish...... - YouTube</u> Raw: https://www.youtube.com/watch?v=ncRi8bZL1q4

49	Link: <u>Most Charitable Countries 2021 (worldpopulationreview.com)</u> Raw: <u>https://worldpopulationreview.com/country-rankings/most-charitable-countries</u>
50	Link: <u>Pingalwara Charitable Society Amritsar - Pingalwara</u> Raw: https://pingalwara.org/
51	Link: <u>KhalsaAid</u> Raw: https://www.khalsaaid.org/
52	When the distinction between "I" and "other" is diminished, you will naturally be concerned for the well-being of others as much as your own. Realise that helping others is helping yourself.
53	Page 299 of PDF, available here: Link: <u>Gurbani Senthia Pothi 4	SGGS Academy</u> Raw: https://sggsacademy.com/download/gurbani-senthia-pothi-4/

Other Useful Resources:

Inequality & Poverty

Link: <u>The Most Persistent Economic Fallacy of All Time! - YouTube</u>
Raw: https://www.youtube.com/watch?v=Hrg1CArkuNc

Link: <u>John Stossel and the fixed Pie Fallacy - YouTube</u>
Raw: https://www.youtube.com/watch?v=jGJ-xHSp5Gc

His tone is somewhat condescending but his points are solid. John Strossel has a good interview here too:

Link: John Stossel - YouTube
Raw: https://www.youtube.com/watch?v=s_oeBBU3xv4

Taxes

Link: Fixing The Way We Tax | Hoover Institution
Raw: https://www.hoover.org/research/fixing-way-we-tax-0

Link: The Case Against Higher Tax Rates | Hoover Institution
Raw: https://www.hoover.org/research/case-against-higher-tax-rates

UBI

Link: The Impact of a Basic Income on Labour Supply and Work Performance (wur.nl)
Raw: https://edepot.wur.nl/373885

Link: Mapped: Where Basic Income Has Been Tested Worldwide (visualcapitalist.com)
Raw: https://www.visualcapitalist.com/map-basic-income-experiments-world/

Link: Everywhere basic income has been tried, in one map: Kenya; Iran; Alaska; Stockton, California; and more - Vox
Raw: https://www.vox.com/future-perfect/2020/2/19/21112570/universal-basic-income-ubi-map

A similar scheme to NIT already exists in the USA in the form of Earned Income Tax Credits. However there are a few key differences:

Link: Bank of England Staff Working Paper No. 903
Raw: https://www.bankofengland.co.uk/-/media/boe/files/working-paper/2021/the-earned-income-tax-credit-targeting-the-poor-but-crowding-out-wealth.pdf

Minimum Wages

Link: IZA World of Labor - Employment effects of minimum wages
Raw: https://wol.iza.org/articles/employment-effects-of-minimum-wages/long

Link: Six Countries with No Minimum Wage | Nomad Capitalist
Raw: https://nomadcapitalist.com/global-citizen/countries-no-minimum-wage/

Link: The American Welfare State: How We Spend Nearly $1 Trillion a Year Fighting Poverty - and fail.pdf (cato.org)
Raw: https://www.cato.org/sites/cato.org/files/pubs/pdf/PA694.pdf

Private Charity

Link: Charity vs. Taxation – What is the Difference? - YouTube
Raw: https://www.youtube.com/watch?v=82NPMM85B6o

Link: Private Charity Beats One-Size-Fits-All Government (reason.com)
Raw: https://reason.com/2020/12/02/private-charity-beats-one-size-fits-all-government/

Link: The 4 Ways to Judge Minimum Wage Laws - Foundation for Economic Education (fee.org)
Raw: https://fee.org/articles/the-4-ways-to-judge-minimum-wage-laws/

Section V
The Role of Government

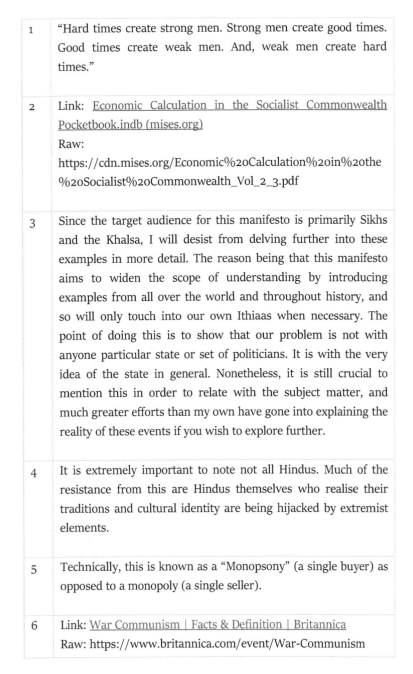

1	"Hard times create strong men. Strong men create good times. Good times create weak men. And, weak men create hard times."
2	Link: <u>Economic Calculation in the Socialist Commonwealth Pocketbook.indb (mises.org)</u> Raw: https://cdn.mises.org/Economic%20Calculation%20in%20the%20Socialist%20Commonwealth_Vol_2_3.pdf
3	Since the target audience for this manifesto is primarily Sikhs and the Khalsa, I will desist from delving further into these examples in more detail. The reason being that this manifesto aims to widen the scope of understanding by introducing examples from all over the world and throughout history, and so will only touch into our own Ithiaas when necessary. The point of doing this is to show that our problem is not with anyone particular state or set of politicians. It is with the very idea of the state in general. Nonetheless, it is still crucial to mention this in order to relate with the subject matter, and much greater efforts than my own have gone into explaining the reality of these events if you wish to explore further.
4	It is extremely important to note not all Hindus. Much of the resistance from this are Hindus themselves who realise their traditions and cultural identity are being hijacked by extremist elements.
5	Technically, this is known as a "Monopsony" (a single buyer) as opposed to a monopoly (a single seller).
6	Link: <u>War Communism	Facts & Definition	Britannica</u> Raw: https://www.britannica.com/event/War-Communism

7	In reality a black market is a free-market, only called "black" because it trades goods and services outlawed by the state.
8	Link: Hanging Order (ibiblio.org) Raw: https://www.ibiblio.org/expo/soviet.exhibit/ad2kulak.html
9	Link: War Communism To NEP : The Road from Serfdom.pdf (mises.org) Raw: https://cdn.mises.org/5_1_5_0.pdf
10	Link: Lenin's New Economic Policy: What it was and how it Changed the Soviet Union - Inquiries Journal Raw: http://www.inquiriesjournal.com/articles/1670/lenins-new-economic-policy-what-it-was-and-how-it-changed-the-soviet-union The above article reports a stance that if Lenin had more time, he could have built up a stronger private sector through the NEP and then gradually transitioned into state-level communism. Azadism views this as a ridiculous excuse since central planning, in general, is fundamentally flawed. It is the wrong direction, no matter how long it takes to get there.
11	China also implemented during their experiments with communism (which led to mass famine and death). Even India post-independence adopted these, and notably, Indira Gandhi during her reign nationalised banks and introduced the "Green Revolution". The devastating effects of such policies can be felt even today. Different formulas have since been used to centrally plan the economy to varying degrees.
12	Link: collectivization	Definition & Facts	Britannica Raw: https://www.ibiblio.org/expo/soviet.exhibit/ad2kulak.html

13	Link: <u>Holodomor survivor tells his story - YouTube</u> Raw: https://www.youtube.com/watch?v=cef_3sfMIGY Link: <u>Jordan Peterson on the Holodomor in Ukraine - YouTube</u> Raw: https://www.youtube.com/watch?v=uGmdZR_Ib7A Link: <u>The Holocaust The New York Times Ignored - YouTube</u> Raw: https://www.youtube.com/watch?v=BqnfmCu6fUk
14	Link: <u>The Legacy of Mao Zedong is Mass Murder	The Heritage Foundation</u> Raw: https://www.heritage.org/asia/commentary/the-legacy-mao-zedong-mass-murder
15	Link: <u>UCLA demographer produces best estimate yet of Cambodia's death toll under Pol Pot	UCLA</u> Raw: https://newsroom.ucla.edu/releases/ucla-demographer-produces-best-estimate-yet-of-cambodias-death-toll-under-pol-pot
16	Link: <u>HRNK_HiddenGulag2_Web_5-18.pdf</u> Raw: https://www.hrnk.org/uploads/pdfs/HRNK_HiddenGulag2_Web_5-18.pdf
17	Link: <u>Satnami's - SikhiWiki, free Sikh encyclopedia.</u> Raw: https://www.sikhiwiki.org/index.php/Satnami%27s Link: <u>The peasant rebels of the Satnami Rebellion (downtoearth.org.in)</u> Raw: https://www.downtoearth.org.in/reviews/the-peasant-rebels-of-the-satnami-rebellion-67044 Link: <u>SATNAMIS OR SADHS: CHANGING IDENTITY OF THE</u>

	SATNAMIS OF NARNAUL on JSTOR Raw: https://www.jstor.org/stable/44148127?item_view=read_onlin e&refreqid=excelsior%3A27c87d70d87c9a792fcdc52a194e6206
18	Link: Do not remain in my presence without Shastar - Guru Gobind Singh Ji (manglacharan.com) Raw: https://www.manglacharan.com/post/do-not-remain-in-my-presence-without-shastar-guru-gobind-singh-ji
19	Link: Shri Akal Takhat - SikhiWiki, free Sikh encyclopedia. Raw: https://www.sikhiwiki.org/index.php/Shri_Akal_Takhat
20	There are multiple variations of this quote as it seems it has likely been passed down as oral tradition rather than in writing. It has been attributed to a Sakhi of when Guru Ji arrived near Ambala: Link: Gurdwara Gobind Pura - SikhiWiki, free Sikh encyclopedia. Raw: https://www.sikhiwiki.org/index.php/Gurdwara_Gobind_Pura Sikh Ri also have good article expanding on the motif of the hawk in Sikhi: Link: Baj: The Hawk and The Sikhs	Harinder Singh	SikhRI Articles Raw: https://sikhri.org/articles/baj-the-hawk-and-the-sikhs
21	Link: A Brief History of Repressive Regimes and Their Gun Laws	Mises Wire Raw: https://mises.org/wire/brief-history-repressive-regimes-and-their-gun-laws

22	Link: <u>FACT CHECK: Did the NRA Support a 1967 'Open Carry' Ban in California? (snopes.com)</u> Raw: https://www.snopes.com/fact-check/nra-california-open-carry-ban/ Hypocrisy is rampant amongst conservative organisations like these, where they may outwardly tout freedom and liberty, however are willing to sacrifice it to meet their own racist agendas. Again, just like corporate lobbying groups like ALEC, this highlights the absurdity of allowing groups like these to lobby government and draft policy.
23	Link: <u>Kashi House Publishing - In the Masters Presence: The Sikhs of Hazoor Sahib</u> Raw: https://www.kashihouse.com/books/in-the-masters-presence-the-sikhs-of-hazoor-sahib-vol-1 Link: ਸੂਖਝੜਗਕੇੜ <u>Kharagket on Twitter:</u> Raw: https://twitter.com/kharagket/status/1209573514526810113?s=21
24	Link: <u>Jhatka Maryada	Jhatka Maryada</u> Raw: http://jhatkamaryada.com/ This is an invaluable resource for knowledge about this topic. They have included countless references from Bani and Ithiaas, completely dismantling the arguments present amongst Sikhs today claiming the Guru's were pro-vegetarian. The reality is that diet has little impact on spirituality, and the Khalsa in particular were actually encouraged to hunt and eat meat. Despite this, even the concept of Jhakta is not in itself that big of an issue. The reason why that whole topic is important is that it acts as a gateway to expanding the view on what Sikhi actually is, and the nuance it contains. It isn't merely a system of blind rituals and by learning the realities of both Bani and Ithiaas, a

	more comprehensive view of what Sikhi is can be established.
25	Link: Budha Dal Misl Nehkalank » 8) Baba Prehlad Singh Ji Raw: https://gb.budhadal.org/baba-prehlad-singh-ji/
26	Giani Ji is amongst the most well-versed scholars of Sikhi in the Panth, learning directly from Jathedar Baba Santa Singh when they were alive. Alongside him, Giani Inderjit Singh Raqbe wale and Giani Gurwinder Singh Nangli are also worth mentioning as great influences to the author for their Katha's and Vichaaran on Sikhi and Ithiaas in Punjabi.
27	A note to MI5/CIA/CID etc. Weapons are a broad definition, weapons is anything used as a tool towards defending oneself or others. This doesn't always mean guns and can refer to other means also. For example, Auranga was killed by the Zafarnamah, a weapon in its own right.
28	Shastar Naam Mala is perhaps the only text of its kind in the sense that every line is praise to different forms of the weapon. Jvala from Manglacharan has a good breakdown of the poetic structure of this composition too, showing the depth of the composition: Link: Layered Meanings in Guru Gobind Singh's Shastar Naam Mala (manglacharan.com) Raw: https://www.manglacharan.com/post/layered-meanings-in-guru-gobind-singh-s-shastar-naam-mala
29	"Sikh Armory" on Instagram are good example of Sikhs taking this seriously: Link: Sikh Armory (@sikharmory) • Instagram photos and videos Raw: https://www.instagram.com/sikharmory/?hl=en

30	It is worth noting, however, that Athens was originally a Monarchy. The monarchs were eventually then deposed and replaced with an oligarchical system of "Archons". Solon is also worthy of note, as an enlightened ruler who paved the way for democracy to later develop. Link: How Athenian Democracy Was Born - Ancient Greece DOCUMENTARY - YouTube Raw: https://www.youtube.com/watch?v=Amu6zhlCJOo
31	Oxford Definition: **Demagoguery** *noun* Political activity or practices that seek support by appealing to the desires and prejudices of ordinary people rather than by using rational argument.
32	Link: Gorgias, by Plato (gutenberg.org) Raw: https://www.gutenberg.org/files/1672/1672-h/1672-h.htm
33	Link: Plato and Socrates warned about populist governments using fear to turn democracies into tyrannies (scroll.in) Raw: https://scroll.in/article/943564/does-not-tyranny-spring-from-democracy-how-platos-380-bc-philosophy-is-truer-than-ever-today
34	Link: Socrates: "I know that I know nothing"	Reason and Meaning Raw: https://reasonandmeaning.com/2019/11/03/socrates-i-know-that-i-know-nothing/ Many of the reasons mentioned here are precisely why Azadism is so averse to central planning. Nobody really knows anything,

	and they for sure do not know how to best manage the lives of others they claim to represent - let alone their economic behaviour! Azadism has the "Socratic humility" to admit that it does not know how to govern your life better than yourself and those around you. This is why it aims to devolve power to the people themselves instead. No central planner is justified to make decisions on your behalf without consent.
35	Jordan Peterson has a lot of content related to the topic of hierarchies if you want to look into them.
36	Again, the Sakhi of the 40 Mukte prove this.
37	Link: America Is a Republic, Not a Democracy | The Heritage Foundation Raw: https://www.heritage.org/american-founders/report/america-republic-not-democracy
38	Link: Adam Smith on Slavery | Adam Smith Works Raw: https://www.adamsmithworks.org/documents/adam-smith-on-slavery
39	Link: Prof. Antony Davies: Why Government Fails, Explained - YouTube Raw: https://www.youtube.com/watch?v=xxmXeLEcs9s This excellent lecture by Anthony Davies completely breaks down the depth of the problem with current political systems. It is crazy to think how this is allowed to persist.
40	All the more reason as to why the Khalsa needs to be at the forefront of this revolution in thinking. Not just copying broken systems of the past and giving it a new paint job to make it "Sikhi themed" - e.g. god forbid, a *Sikh Soviet Union.*

41	Link: Joscha Bach: Nature of Reality, Dreams, and Consciousness | Lex Fridman Podcast #212 - YouTube Raw: https://www.youtube.com/watch?v=rIpUf-Vy2JA&list=FLvvK7-jiFYuwqHye866xRVA&index=5 The above is an interview with Joscha Bach who is a cognitive scientist, AI researcher and philosopher. I felt the accuracy of some of his statements here is very high when compared against the assessment of reality by Dharmic traditions (of which Sikhi is one). The whole interview is an interesting and fun observation in how the same reality described by the Gurus and other great Mahapurakh through a Dharmic lexicon of terminology can be also be described in "computer-sciencey" terminology by modern philosophers and scientists today. It's also interesting watching the west adopt terms from fields like computer science since everyday language was not designed to explore the depth of Paramatma. After a point, even this may fail and it should be the Khalsa (and Dharmic traditions in general) there to help fill in the gaps. But even then this only extends the inevitable. After a while, all language fails and only experience of that one existence is appropriate. The words are just stepping stones to help us to the other side.
42	The ultimate culmination of spiritual practice. Enlightenment itself.
43	A future effort may be conducted to research and outline in more detail, a modern Sikhi-based guidance on these matters. A sort of rules of engagement for the Khalsa.
44	If a tax system is still maintained at this point, then this can be more difficult. A means by which to decide who gets the tax would have to be established. However, the best is just a donation or Dasvandh-based system to ensure freedom. Alternatively, this could be devolved to city or locality levels and each population decides collectively which Misl to pay. Again, not ideal but in the right direction at least. Further Vichaar can

	be done here in future.
45	It would also give the media something to report on.
46	Obviously, not everyone has to own weapons, it's up to them. Some may want to follow different lifestyles and that's fine too. But for the Khalsa, it's their duty as Kshatriyae to safeguard them if they request help, just as the duty (or Dharam) of a Kshatriya in ancient India was to protect the Brahmins and other castes.
47	A notable occurrence of a wrestling match of this nature in Ithiaas was the one mentioned in Panth Prakash. Read episode 73 available here: Link: Sri Gur Panth Prakash Volume 1 (Episodes 1 to 81) Raw: https://archive.org/details/SriGurPanthPrakashVolume1episodes1To81/page/447/mode/2up?
48	In fact the only nation to succeed in subduing the region was Maharaja Ranjit Singh's empire.
49	This should not be confused with praise of the Taliban. They are still the same Turks and Malechh the Singhs fought and subdued in the past.
50	For more information, please consult his book: Link: Democracy: The God That Failed	Mises Institute Raw:https://mises.org/library/democracy-god-failed-1
51	The best Raag.

52	Chankyaniti, Shahnama, Hitopadesha to name a few. Even Guru Gobind Singh's own composition, Charitropakhyan, is a good example.
53	Must be noted that a lie that deserves a punishment are only those in which it causes material harm as to be determine in court of law. For example a company lying about the safety of their products or employer lying about how much salary they would pay. Lies of lesser weight would be hard to determine if they have no effect, and it is unreasonable to shut down freedom of speech over certain things. If someone says something that is disagreeable but causes no material harm (hurt feelings do not count) then how can we distinguish between an opinion and a lie? Therefore, only those lies are punishable that can be provably shown to break the NAP. Additionally, lying in general is a form of self-sabotage. Once the people inevitably find out, then all trust is lost and any market interactions with the liar are likely to cease anyway. Only in systems such as the ones present in politics actually reward and prop up liars.
54	In fact, much of this effort was inspired by Bhai Jugraj Singh themselves. They not only delved into the basics of Sikh philosophy but produced many videos and lectures on political elements and the sort of directions the Khalsa should take in the 21st century.
55	Danish researcher and Sikh scholar Satnam Singh mentions this insight in an incredible lecture he gave, available here: Link: Crushing pride through the Japji Sahib by Satnam Singh, University of Warwick - YouTube Raw:https://www.youtube.com/watch?v=VF1dXGdqTWc

56	However, there is apparently a clause that stipulates that Muslims should follow the laws of the land in non-Muslim nations. If so, adhering to the NAP should not be a problem under an Azadist nation.
57	One of the reasons why I say this is because in Guru Gobind Singh's composition 'Ugardanti' he makes mention of the Khalsa being the Tisarpanth (third way), distinct from both (Brahmanical) Hinduism and Islam. However, compared with Guru Nanak's statement of there being 'no Hindu and no Muslim', to me, I interpret both Sikhi and the Khalsa as distinct (although related). Not all Sikhs are Khalsa, but all Khalsa are fundamentally Sikh. Sikhi is therefore a more broad, spiritual identity that transcends religion, whereas the Khalsa is more grounded in religious sentiment. As stated in the main body, it is just one particular way of practising Sikhi as sanctioned by the Guru themselves.
58	But even then, some Singh's are Niyare and in complete Masti. They give no mind to what is permitted by the state or not, nor would they be worried about punishment either. That doesn't mean they won't be punished, it just means that the Nihang Singh probably wouldn't care and do it anyway. But to maintain punishment for those things and still recognise it as a crime is crucial for the general law and order in a society. Hopefully, though many of these types of Singh would be in a government Misl anyway under the watch of a Jathedar/Misldar and bound to a set of Rehits. This then allows this energy to be channelled against real enemies instead.

Other Useful Resources:

Link: Russia's Last Capitalists (cdlib.org)
Raw:
https://publishing.cdlib.org/ucpressebooks/view?docId=ft2199n7h5;chunk.id=0;doc.view=print

Link: <u>An economic history of the U.S.S.R. : Nove, Alec : Free Download, Borrow, and Streaming : Internet Archive</u>
Raw:https://archive.org/details/economichistoryooonove/page/54/mode/2 up?q=black+market&view=theater

Link: <u>Ukraine - Ukraine in the interwar period | Britannica</u>
Raw: https://www.britannica.com/place/Ukraine/Ukraine-in-the-interwar-period

Link: <u>The Atrocities That Nobody Knows About - YouTube</u>
Raw: https://www.youtube.com/watch?v=t9xrmJ3UX9w

Link: <u>Nazinsky: Stalin's Cannibal Island - YouTube</u>
Raw:
https://www.youtube.com/watch?v=CaOwcYLGTMo&list=PLxUfDdw5RjEJc _uuNrkXyNgUHonoTP6L8&index=4

See Chapter 10 - Why the worst get on top (page 26 of PDF):

Link: <u>Road To Serfdom (mises.org)</u>
Raw: https://cdn.mises.org/Road%20to%20serfdom.pdf

Glossary

The author's own interpretations has been used for many these words, since often the definitions fall short. The Mahan Kosh is also a good resource to consult for definitions and meanings also.

Word	Meaning
Atma	Commonly translated as soul, consciousness, mind. However, this is perhaps more accurately described as the "separateness" from God or the distinct individual part of God that is embedded in a separate self.
Bani	Meaning speech, utterance. Used in this manifesto as short for Gurbani.
Bhagat	One who does Bhagti, devotional worship of God.
Bhavani	One of the expressions of God in a feminine form with particular emphasis on the life giving qualities. Creative energy of God.
Bir Ras	Warrior spirit/essence. To be imbued with Bir Ras is to adopt a mindset willing to engage in battle.
Brahm	Short for Brahma
Brahma	One of the 3 principle deities in Hindu mythology. Brahma is the creator god, symbolising the creative aspects of God. Often in Bani this can be used interchangeably as a term for God.
Brahmgy aan	Knowledge and wisdom of Brahma/God
Darbar	Royal court that brings together musicians, poets, philosophers and others into a single space to highlight excellence in each field or to hold discussions. Generally under the patronage of a monarch or noble.
Dastar	Turban
Dasvandh	Translated as "tenth part". This is a practice amongst Sikhs to pay 10% of their earnings towards charity, the community or the Khalsa and the Guru.
Dharam	Righteousness or Duty. When Hanuman sneaked into Lanka and found Sita, she refused to go back with him to Raam. The reason being that she wanted to give Raam

	the opportunity to fulfil his Dharam, as it was his duty to rescue her. Dharam also refers to the spiritual traditions of India as well.
Ghulami	Slavery, oppression
Giani	Someone who is wise and knowledgeable about Sikhi. Often referred to a "priestly" role.
God	Commonly referred to as VahiGuru in Sikh tradition. God in Sikhi is not referring to a cloud wizard. Instead, it is understood as existence itself. In love for God, certain personified qualities are attributed to it which aids in reaching enlightenment (oneness or realisation of the nature of existence/reality). God is therefore everything in existence. There is nothing but God.
Gurbani	Speech, utterances, writings of the Guru
Guru	Gu = Darkness, Ru = Light. Hence a Guru is that which brings light (symbolising knowledge/wisdom) to dispel the darkness (ignorance). An "enlightener".
Gurudwara	A building that houses the Guru. Acts as a place of worship
Gyaan	Wisdom, knowledge
Hari	A name for God.
Haumai	I,me - the feeling of a separate sense of self
Hukam	Order. This refers to "God's will" or the natural predetermined set of events ordained by God
Ik Onkaar	Non-duality. Ik - refers to the number one, as to avoid any misinterpretation. Oan/Om - the first breakdown of that one to help understand it. It is made up of 3 syllables - A, U, M which each symbolise the waking state of consciousness, dream state, and dreamless sleep state. This covers all possible layers of reality, thereby symbolising that this Ik, is indeed present in every aspect of existence. The Kaar further reminds us of this as it symbolises the Ik present in all three states of consciousness (Turiya). There are other breakdowns of this such as the creation and expansion of existence or the Trimurti version, however, they all pertain to the

	same thing - that all reality is essentially the same thing - "thingness" itself. Ik Onkaar highlights the non-dualism of Sikh philosophy, and all of Gurbani is designed to explain it and how to transcend the illusion that we are separate from it.
Jagat	World - hence Jagat Guru means the Guru for the whole world
Japu ji Sahib	The first section of the Guru Granth Sahib, written by Guru Nanak and read daily by Sikhs
Jhatka	A method of killing in one blow or shot as to avoid any unnecessary suffering and cruelty
Ji	Term of respect
Kali	One of the expressions of God in a feminine form with particular emphasis on rage and destruction of enemies in battle.
Kalyug	Age of darkness, iron age - In Hindu mythology the surface level interpretation is referring to the period of immoral behaviour and a lack of societal ethics. However, on a deeper level, it can refer to one's own state of mind
Kamarkas sa	A waistband
Karma	Action - can refer to the laws of cause and effect. Put your foot in a puddle and it gets wet.
Khalsa	One of the original expressions of Sikhi as a religion. This refers to the order of warrior saints established by Guru Gobind Singh in 1699. The Guru aimed to turn many of his Sikhs into saint-soldiers in order to fight oppression and tyranny.
Khande Di Pahul	Referring to the Amrit given during the ceremony that initiates a Sikh into the Khalsa Panth. This was the original term used for this.
Khoj	To search and uncover (knowledge)
Langar	A tradition established by Guru Nanak that refers to the free community kitchen that feeds all regardless of any caste, religion, background or other arbitrary labels.
Laxmi	One of the expressions of God in a feminine form with

	particular emphasis on wealth and prosperity.
Mahapur akh	A great being - referring to those people who have successfully overcome the illusion of separateness and have become enlightened. They are "one with God".
Maharaja	A King or Emperor
Mahesh	Another name for Shiva
Maya	Refers to the material, physical reality. It is also referred to as the illusion of separateness from God. However, it is still God. The illusion still exists, it's just a matter of perception. When discussing the topics of this manifesto (and most things in general), these are in the illusion.
Miri	Temporal/worldly matters.
Nirbhau	Without fear
Nirvair	Without hate
Pankti	A line from Gurbani
Panth	The (Sikh) path/community
Paramat ma	Supreme Atma. Another word for God
Parchar	Preaching or educating others, generally about spirituality
Piri	Spiritual matters
Prabhu	Another word for God
Raag	or Ragas - a specific mood. This refers to the system of Indian classical music, of which Gurbani is divided by.
Raagi	One who plays music in Raag
Raaj	(Political) Rule
Raam Chandar	The mythological hero in the Ramayan. He acts as metaphor for God as well as Dharam (duty). The Sikh Gurus are also decended from his line as is reveled in Guru Gobind Singh's Bachittar Natak from Dassam Granth
Raja	Short for Maharaja (also can be a lower rank monarch)
Ramayan	One of the main Ithiaas in Vedic traditions. Guru Gobind Singh also has his own version: 'Ram Avtar', which is a translated version of the original but with more emphasis

	on the Bir Ras components of the story.
Sakhi	Story
Salok	A type of poetic verse
Sama	Time, situation, period
Sant	Saint
Sant Sipahi	Saint Soldier
Sarup	A form. Used commonly to refer to a physical copy of Sri Guru Granth Sahib
Satyug	Age of truth, Golden age - In Hindu mythology the surface level interpretation is referring to the period of enlightenment and a society that is completely in tune with its spirituality. However, on a deeper level, it can refer to one's own state of mind
Seva	(selfless) service - often referring to charitable actions
Sevak	One who does Seva
Shabad	word(s) of the Guru - often referring to hymns, verses and sections in the Guru Granth Sahib
Shaheed	Martyr - one who overcomes their innate instinct of self-preservation (embedded through millions of years of evolution) in order to uphold the preservation of the life and property of others above his own.
Shastar	Weapons
Shastardhari	One who keeps armed
Shikaar	Hunting
Shiva	One of the 3 principle deities in Hindu mythology. Shiva is the destroyer god, symbolising the destructive aspects of God. In order for new things to arise, the old must be destroyed (altered, changed). Sometimes in Bani this can be used interchangeably as a term for God.
Siddha	A type of hermit or ascetic
Sikhi	Sikhism - the spiritual framework as established by Guru Nanak. Sikhi itself isn't a religion, as it is merely the set of teachings that can be adopted and understood by all

	humanity without obligation. The Khalsa can be seen as one of the religions of Sikhi (alongside Udasin, Nirmale, Sevapanthi etc). Sikhi can be practised either with religion or without.
Sikhiya	A teaching, lessons
Simran	Remembrance - referring to a meditative practice that put focus on God
Sipahi	Soldier
Sita	The wife of Raam Chandar. Can also symbolise the self.
Sri	Term of respect
Tapasya	Focused, dedicated form of meditation
Tulwar	A type of sword
Upashana	Devotion
Upashik	Devotee
Updesh	A teaching (from a Guru)
Vedanta	One of the six main schools of Hindu mythology, primarily dealing with the Upanishads
Vichaar	Contemplation
Vishnu	One of the 3 principal deities in Hindu mythology. Vishnu is the sustainer god, symbolising the aspects of God involved with maintaining existence. Vishnu is often incarnated as Avtars in many Ithiaas. Sometimes in Bani this can be used interchangeably as a term for God.
Yogi	Practitioner of Yoga - someone seeking union with God

Economic Freedom

Assessing Azadism against the Index of Economic Freedom

The Index of Economic Freedom is an annual ranking maintained by the Heritage Foundation. Through a variety of factors and measures, it aims to determine the level of economic freedom across the world. The following is from the Foundation's website, describing their definitions:

Q.1. What is economic freedom?

Economic freedom is the fundamental right of every human to control his or her own labor and property. In an economically free society, individuals are free to work, produce, consume, and invest in any way they please. In economically free societies, governments allow labor, capital, and goods to move freely, and refrain from coercion or constraint of liberty beyond the extent necessary to protect and maintain liberty itself.

Azadism interprets that last line as the ability to uphold the Non-Aggression Principle (NAP) as a vital component in maintaining a free and fair market. Economic freedom is just a particular emphasis on freedom in general since a society can not be free without also being economically free. Through this freedom, innovation and human ingenuity can remain unrestricted as people can decide to live their lives in the way that they chose for themselves, as opposed to state coercion. However much a state trends towards freedom, the greater the benefit in terms of prosperity and human rights. This index helps understand the key components to consider when assessing the types of policies to employ to maximise these conditions and avoid tyranny and an erosion of human freedom.

For more information about the index, please see their website:

Link: 2021 Index of Economic Freedom | The Heritage Foundation
Raw: https://www.heritage.org/index/about

The index measures economic freedom by splitting it into 4 sections, namely:

1. Rule of Law (property rights, government integrity, judicial effectiveness)

2. Government Size (government spending, tax burden, fiscal health)

3. Regulatory Efficiency (business freedom, labour freedom, monetary freedom)

4. Open Markets (trade freedom, investment freedom, financial freedom)

Their annual report contains a section on the methodology that further details each of these measures. Let's assess how Azadism views each category and what it aims to increase or reduce:

Rule of Law	Azadism Bias	Government Size	Azadism Bias	Regulatory Efficiency	Azadism Bias	Open Markets	Azadism Bias
Property rights	Strong	Government spending	Minimal (if at all)	Business freedom	High	Trade freedom	High
Government integrity	Strong	Tax burden	Minimal (if at all)	Labour freedom	High	Investment freedom	High
Judicial effectiveness	Strong	Fiscal health	Strong (any surplus, give back)	Monetary freedom	High	Financial freedom	High

Printed in Poland
by Amazon Fulfillment
Poland Sp. z o.o., Wrocław